L A W
Services

- **The Official**

LSAT

TriplePrep™ —Volume 1

Bantam Doubleday Dell

Published by
Bantam Doubleday Dell Publishing Group, Inc.
1540 Broadway
New York, New York 10036

Library of Congress Cataloging in Publication Data
LSAT: *The Official Tripleprep*
p. cm.

"A publication of Law School Admission Services/Law School Admission Council."

ISBN 0-385-31288-1 (v. 1).—ISBN 0-385-31291-1 (v. 2)

1. Law School Admission Test.   2. Law schools—United States—Admission.
I. Law School Admission Services (U.S.) II. Law School Admission Council.
KF285.Z9L782 1994
340'.076—dc20
                                                    94-4303
                                                    CIP

Manufactured in the United States of America
Published simultaneously in Canada

June 1994

10 9 8 7 6 5 4 3 2 1

The Law School Admission Test is a half-day standardized test required for admission to all 191 LSAC-member law schools. It consists of five 35-minute sections of multiple-choice questions. Four of the five sections contribute to the test taker's score. These sections include one reading comprehension section, one analytical reasoning section, and two logical reasoning sections. The fifth section typically is used to pretest new test items and to preequate new test forms. A 30-minute writing sample is administered at the end of the test. The writing sample is not scored by Law Services; however, copies of the writing sample are sent to all law schools to which you apply. The score scale for the LSAT is 120 to 180, with 120 being the lowest possible score and 180 the highest possible score.

The LSAT is designed to measure skills that are considered essential for success in law school: the reading and comprehension of complex texts with accuracy and insight; the organization and management of information and the ability to draw reasonable inferences from it; the ability to reason critically; and the analysis and evaluation of the reasoning and argument of others.

The LSAT provides a standard measure of acquired reading and verbal reasoning skills that law schools can use as one of several factors in assessing applicants.

Scoring

Your LSAT score is based on the number of questions you answer correctly (the raw score). There is no deduction for incorrect answers, and all questions count equally. In other words, there is no penalty for guessing.

■ Test Score Accuracy—Reliability and Standard Error of Measurement

Candidates perform at different levels on different occasions for reasons quite unrelated to the characteristics of a test itself. The accuracy of test scores is best described by the use of two related statistical terms, reliability and standard error of measurement.

Reliability is a measure of how consistently a test measures the skills under investigation. The higher the reliability coefficient for a test, the more certain we can be that test takers would get very similar scores if they took the test again.

Law Services reports an internal consistency measure of reliability for every test form. The reliability coefficient can vary from 0.00 to 1.00; a test with no measurement error would have a reliability coefficient of 1.00 (never attained in practice). In the past, reliability coefficients for LSAT forms have ranged from .90 to .95, indicating a very reliable test. Law Services expects the reliability to continue to fall within the same range.

The LSAT, like any standardized test, is not a perfect measuring instrument. One way to quantify measurement error is through calculation of the **standard error of measurement**. The standard error of measurement provides an estimate of the error that is present in a test score because of the imperfect reliability of the test.

The standard error of measurement for the LSAT is reported to score users following each administration of the test. The chances are approximately two out of three that a score obtained by a test taker will lie within a range from one standard error of measurement below to one standard error of measurement above his or her true score; true score is the score that a test taker would have obtained if the test were perfectly reliable. About 95 percent of the test takers will have test scores that fall within two standard errors of measurement of their true scores. The standard error of measurement for LSAT forms tends to be approximately 2.5.

Measurement error also must be taken into account when comparing LSAT scores of two test takers. It is likely that small differences in scores are due to measurement error rather than to meaningful differences in ability. The standard error of score differences provides some guidance as to the importance of differences between two scores. The standard error of score differences is approximately 1.4 times as large as the standard error of measurement for the individual scores.

Thus, a test score should be regarded as a useful but approximate measure of a candidate's abilities as measured by the test, not as an exact determination of his or her standing. LSAS encourages law schools to interpret LSAT scores as intervals, not as exact points on a scale.

■ Adjustments for Variation in Test Difficulty

All test forms of the LSAT reported on the same score scale are designed to measure the same abilities, but one test form may be slightly easier or harder than another. The scores from different test forms are made comparable through a statistical procedure known as equating. As a result of equating, a given scaled score earned on different test forms reflects the same level of ability.

■ Research on the LSAT

Summaries of LSAT validity studies and other LSAT research can be found in member law school libraries.

How the PrepTest Differs from an Actual LSAT

Each PrepTest is made up of the scored sections and writing sample from an actual LSAT. However, it does not contain the extra, variable section that is used to pre-test new test items of one of the three question types. Also, you are likely to encounter the three LSAT question types in a different order when you take an actual LSAT than in the PrepTest. This is because the order of the question types is intentionally varied for each administration of the test.

The Question Types

The multiple-choice questions that make up most of the LSAT reflect a broad range of academic disciplines and are intended to give no advantage to candidates from a particular academic background.

The five sections of the test contain three different question types. The following material presents a general discussion of the nature of each question type and some strategies that can be used in answering them.

■ Reading Comprehension Questions

The purpose of reading comprehension questions is to measure your ability to read, with understanding and insight, examples of lengthy and complex materials similar to those commonly encountered in law school work. The reading comprehension section of the test consists of four passages, each approximately 450 words long, followed by five to eight questions that test the candidate's reading and reasoning abilities. Passages for reading comprehension items draw from a variety of subjects—including the humanities, the social sciences, the physical sciences, ethics, philosophy, and the law.

Reading comprehension questions require test takers to read carefully and accurately, to determine the relationships among the various parts of the passage, and to draw reasonable inferences from the material in the passage. The questions may ask about:

- the main idea or primary purpose of the passage;

- the meaning or purpose of words or phrases used in the passage;

- information explicitly stated in the passage;

- information or ideas that can be inferred from the passage;

- the organization of the passage;

- the application of information in the passage to a new context; and

- the tone of the passage or the author's attitude as it is revealed in the language used.

Suggested Approach

Since passages are drawn from many different disciplines and sources, you should not be discouraged if you encounter material with which you are not familiar. It is important to remember that questions are to be answered on the basis of the information provided in the passage. There is no particular knowledge that you are expected to bring to the test, and you should not make inferences based on any prior knowledge of a subject that you may have. You may, however, wish to defer working on a passage that seems particularly difficult or unfamiliar until after you have dealt with passages you find easier.

Strategies. In preparing for the test, you should experiment with different strategies, and decide which work most effectively for you. These include:

- Reading the passage very closely and then answering the questions;

- Reading the questions first, reading the passage closely, and then returning to the questions; and

- Skimming the passage and questions very quickly, then rereading the passage closely and answering the questions.

Remember that your strategy must be effective under timed conditions.

Reading the passage. Whatever strategy you choose, you should give the passage at least one careful reading before answering the questions. Separate main ideas from supporting ideas and the author's own ideas or attitudes from factual, objective information. Note transitions from one idea to the next and examine the relationships among the different ideas or parts of the passage. For example, are they contrasting or complementary? Consider how and why the author makes points and draws conclusions. Be sensitive to the implications of what the passage says.

You may find it helpful to mark key parts of the passage. For example, you might underline main ideas or important arguments, and you might circle transitional words—'although,' 'nevertheless,' 'correspondingly,' and the like—that will help you map the structure of the passage. Moreover, you might note descriptive words that will help you identify the author's attitude toward a particular idea or person.

Answering the Questions

- Always read all the answer choices before selecting the best answer. The best answer choice is the one that most accurately and completely answers the question being posed.

- Respond to the specific question being asked. Do not pick an answer choice simply because it is a true statement. For example, picking a true statement might yield an incorrect answer to a question in which you are asked to identify the author's position on an issue, since here you are not being asked to evaluate the truth of the author's position, but only to correctly identify what that position is.

- Answer the questions only on the basis of the information provided in the passage. Your own views, interpretations, or opinions, and those you have heard from others, may sometimes conflict with those expressed in the passage; however, you are expected to work within the context provided by the passage. You should not expect to agree with everything you encounter in reading comprehension passages.

■ Analytical Reasoning Questions

Analytical reasoning items are designed to measure the ability to understand a structure of relationships and to draw conclusions about the structure. The examinee is asked to make deductions from a set of statements, rules, or conditions that describe relationships among entities such as persons, places, things, or events. They simulate the kinds of detailed analyses of relationships that a law student must perform in solving legal problems. For example, a passage might describe four diplomats sitting around a table, following certain rules of protocol as to who can sit where. The test taker must answer questions about the implications of the given information, for example, who is sitting between diplomats X and Y.

The passage used for each group of questions describes a common relationship such as the following:

- Assignment: Two parents, P and O, and their children, R and S, must go to the dentist on four consecutive days, designated 1, 2, 3, and 4 ...;

- Ordering: X arrived before Y but after Z;

- Grouping: A basketball coach is trying to form a lineup from seven players— R,S,T,U,V,W, and X...and each player has a particular strength—shooting, jumping, or guarding;

- Spatial: Country X contains six cities and each city is connected to at least one other city by a system of roads, some of which are one-way.

Careful reading and analysis are necessary to determine the exact nature of the relationships involved. Some relationships are fixed (e.g., P and R always sit at the same table). Other relationships are variable (e.g., Q must be assigned to either table 1 or table 3). Some relationships that are not stated in the conditions are implied by and can be deduced from those that are stated. (e.g., If one condition about books on a shelf specifies that Book L is to the left of Book Y, and another specifies that Book P is to the left of Book L, then it can be deduced that Book P is to the left of Book Y.)

No formal training in logic is required to answer these questions correctly. Analytical reasoning questions are intended to be answered using knowledge, skills, and reasoning ability generally expected of college students and graduates.

Suggested Approach

Some people may prefer to answer first those questions about a passage that seem less difficult and then those that seem more difficult. In general, it is best not to start another passage before finishing one begun earlier, because much time can be lost in returning to a passage and reestablishing familiarity with its relationships. Do not assume that, because the conditions for a set of questions look long or complicated, the questions based on those conditions will necessarily be especially difficult.

Reading the passage. In reading the conditions, do not introduce unwarranted assumptions. For instance, in a set establishing relationships of height and weight among the members of a team, do not assume that a person who is taller than another person must weigh more than that person. All the information needed to answer each question is provided in the passage and the question itself.

The conditions are designed to be as clear as possible; do not interpret them as if they were intended to trick you. For example, if a question asks how many people could be eligible to serve on a committee, consider only those people named in the passage unless directed otherwise. When in doubt, read the conditions in their most obvious sense. Remember, however, that the language in the conditions is intended to be read for precise meaning. It is essential to pay particular attention to words that describe or limit relationships, such as 'only,' 'exactly,' 'never,' 'always,' 'must be,' 'cannot be,' and the like.

The result of this careful reading will be a clear picture of the structure of the relationships involved, including the kinds of relationships permitted, the participants in the relationships, and the range of actions or attributes allowed by the relationships for these participants.

Questions are independent. Each question should be considered separately from the other questions in its group; no information, except what is given in the original conditions, should be carried over from one question to another. In some cases a question will simply ask for conclusions to be drawn from the conditions as originally given. Some questions may, however, add information to the original conditions or temporarily suspend one of the original conditions for the purpose of that question only. For example, if Question 1 adds the information "if P is sitting at table 2...," this information should NOT be carried over to any other question in the group.

Highlighting the text; using diagrams. Many people find it useful to underline key points in the passage and in each question. In addition, it may prove very helpful to draw a diagram to assist you in finding the solution to the problem.

In preparing for the test, you may wish to experiment with different types of diagrams. For a scheduling problem, a calendar-like diagram may be helpful. For a spatial relationship problem, a simple map can be a useful device.

Even though some people find diagrams to be very helpful, other people seldom use them. And among those who do regularly use diagrams in solving these problems, there is by no means universal agreement on which kind of diagram is best for which problem or in which cases a diagram is most useful. Do not be concerned if a particular problem in the test seems to be best approached without the use of a diagram.

■ Logical Reasoning Questions

Logical reasoning questions evaluate a test taker's ability to understand, analyze, criticize, and complete arguments. The arguments are contained in short passages taken from a variety of sources, including letters to the editor, speeches, advertisements, newspaper articles and editorials, informal discussions and conversations, as well as articles in the humanities, the social sciences, and the natural sciences.

Each logical reasoning question requires the examinee to read and comprehend the argument or the reasoning

contained in the passage, and answer one or two questions about it. The questions test a variety of logical skills. These include:

- recognizing the point or issue of an argument or dispute;

- detecting the assumptions involved in an argument or chain of reasoning;

- drawing reasonable conclusions from given evidence or premises;

- identifying and applying principles;

- identifying the method or structure of an argument or chain of reasoning;

- detecting reasoning errors and misinterpretations;

- determining how additional evidence or argument affects an argument or conclusion; and

- identifying explanations and recognizing resolutions of conflicting facts or arguments.

The questions do not presuppose knowledge of the terminology of formal logic. For example, you will not be expected to know the meaning of specialized terms such as "ad hominem" or "syllogism." On the other hand, you will be expected to understand and critique the reasoning contained in arguments. This requires that you possess, at a minimum, a college-level understanding of widely used concepts such as argument, premise, assumption, and conclusion.

Suggested Approach

Read each question carefully. Make sure that you understand the meaning of each part of the question. Make sure that you understand the meaning of each answer choice and the ways in which it may or may not relate to the question posed.

Do not pick a response simply because it is a true statement. Although true, it may not answer the question posed.

Answer each question on the basis of the information that is given, even if you do not agree with it. Work within the context provided by the passage. LSAT questions do not involve any tricks or hidden meanings.

The Writing Exercise

Test takers are given 30 minutes to complete the brief writing exercise, which is not scored but is used by law school admission personnel to assess writing skill. Read the topic carefully. You will probably find it best to spend a few minutes considering the topic and organizing your thoughts before you begin writing. **Do not write on a topic other than the one specified. Writing on a topic of your own choice is not acceptable.**

There is no "right" or "wrong" position on the writing sample topic. Law schools are interested in how skillfully you support the position you take and how clearly you express that position. How well you write is much more important than how much you write. No special knowledge is required or expected. Law schools are interested in organization, vocabulary, and writing mechanics. They understand the short time available to you and the pressure under which you are writing.

Confine your writing to the lined area following the writing sample topic. You will find that you have enough space if you plan your writing carefully, write on every line, avoid wide margins, and keep your handwriting a reasonable size. Be sure that your handwriting is legible.

Scratch paper is provided for use during the writing sample portion of the test only. Scratch paper cannot be used in other sections of the LSAT.

The writing sample is photocopied and sent to law schools to which you direct your LSAT score. A pen will be provided at the test center, which must be used (for the writing sample only) to ensure a photocopy of high quality.

Taking the PrepTest Under Simulated LSAT Conditions

One important way to prepare for the LSAT is to take a sample test under the same requirements and time limits you will encounter in taking an actual LSAT. This helps you to estimate the amount of time you can afford to spend on each question in a section and to determine the question types on which you may need additional practice.

Since the LSAT is a timed test, it is important to use your allotted time wisely. During the test, you may work only on the section designated by the test supervisor. You cannot devote extra time to a difficult section and make up that time on a section you find easier. In pacing yourself, and checking your answers, you should think of each section of the test as a separate minitest.

Be sure that you answer every question on the test. When you do not know the correct answer to a question, first eliminate the responses that you know are incorrect, then make your best guess among the remaining choices. Do not be afraid to guess.

When you take a sample test abide by all the requirements specified in the directions and keep strictly within the specified time limits. Work without a rest period. When you take an actual test you will have only a short break—usually 10-15 minutes—after SECTION III.

When taken under conditions as much like actual testing conditions as possible, a sample test provides very useful preparation for taking the LSAT.

Official directions for the four multiple-choice sections and the writing sample are included in this book so that you can use the PrepTests to approximate actual testing conditions as you practice.

To take a sample test:

- Set a timer for 35 minutes. Answer all the questions in SECTION I of one PrepTest. Stop working on that section when the 35 minutes have elapsed.

- Repeat, allowing yourself 35 minutes each for sections II, III, and IV.

- Set the timer for 30 minutes, then prepare your response to the writing sample for the PrepTest.

- Refer to "Computing Your Score" for that PrepTest for instruction on evaluating your performance. An answer key is provided for that purpose.

LAW Services

■ **The Official**

LSAT

PrepTest™ II

The sample test that follows consists of
four sections corresponding to the four
scored sections of the October 1991 LSAT.

October 1991
Form 2LSS12

General Directions for the LSAT Answer Sheet

The actual testing time for this portion of the test will be 2 hours 55 minutes. There are five sections, each with a time limit of 35 minutes. The supervisor will tell you when to begin and end each section. If you finish a section before time is called, you may check your work on that section only; do not turn to any other section of the test book and do not work on any other section either in the test book or on the answer sheet.

There are several different types of questions on the test, and each question type has its own directions. Be sure you understand the directions for each question type before attempting to answer any questions in that section.

Not everyone will finish all the questions in the time allowed. Do not hurry, but work steadily and as quickly as you can without sacrificing accuracy. You are advised to use your time effectively. If a question seems too difficult, go on to the next one and return to the difficult question after completing the section. MARK THE BEST ANSWER YOU CAN FOR EVERY QUESTION. NO DEDUCTIONS WILL BE MADE FOR WRONG ANSWERS. YOUR SCORE WILL BE BASED ONLY ON THE NUMBER OF QUESTIONS YOU ANSWER CORRECTLY.

ALL YOUR ANSWERS MUST BE MARKED ON THE ANSWER SHEET. Answer spaces for each question are lettered to correspond with the letters of the potential answers to each question in the test book. After you have decided which of the answers is correct, blacken the corresponding space on the answer sheet. BE SURE THAT EACH MARK IS BLACK AND COMPLETELY FILLS THE ANSWER SPACE. Give only one answer to each question. If you change an answer, be sure that all previous marks are erased completely. Since the answer sheet is machine scored, incomplete erasures may be interpreted as intended answers. ANSWERS RECORDED IN THE TEST BOOK WILL NOT BE SCORED.

There may be more questions noted on this answer sheet than there are questions in a section. Do not be concerned but be certain that the section and number of the question you are answering matches the answer sheet section and question number. Additional answer spaces in any answer sheet section should be left blank. Begin your next section in the number one answer space for that section.

Score Cancellation

Complete this section only if you are absolutely certain you want to cancel your score. A CANCELLATION REQUEST CANNOT BE RESCINDED. IF YOU ARE AT ALL UNCERTAIN, YOU SHOULD NOT COMPLETE THIS SECTION; INSTEAD, YOU SHOULD USE THE TIME ALLOWED AFTER THE TEST (UP TO 5 DAYS) TO FULLY CONSIDER YOUR DECISION.

To cancel your score from this administration, you must:

A.　fill in the ovals here........　◯ ◯

B.　read the following statement. Then sign your name and enter the date.

I certify that I wish to cancel my test score from this administration. I understand that my request is irreversible and that my score will not be sent to me or to the law schools to which I apply.

_____

Sign your name in full

_____

Date

HOW DID YOU PREPARE FOR THE LSAT?
(Select all that apply.)

Responses to this item are voluntary and will be used for statistical research purposes only.

◯ By studying the sample questions in the LSAT/LSDAS Registration and Information Book.
◯ By taking the free sample LSAT.
◯ By working through The Official LSAT PrepTest(s), PrepBook, Workbooks, or PrepKit.
◯ By using a book on how to prepare for the LSAT not published by Law Services.
◯ By attending a commercial test preparation or coaching course.
◯ By attending a test preparation or coaching course offered through an undergraduate institution.
◯ Self study.
◯ Other preparation.
◯ No preparation.

CERTIFYING STATEMENT

Please write (DO NOT PRINT) the following statement. Sign and date.

I certify that I am the examinee whose name appears on this answer sheet and that I am here to take the LSAT for the sole purpose of being considered for admission to law school. I further certify that I will neither assist nor receive assistance from any other candidate, and I agree not to copy or retain examination questions or to transmit them in any form to any other person.

_____

_____

_____

_____

_____

_____

_____

_____

_____

SIGNATURE: _____　TODAY'S DATE: ___ / ___ / ___
　　　　　　　　　　　　　　　　　　　　　　　　　MONTH　DAY　YEAR

INSTRUCTIONS FOR COMPLETING THE BIOGRAPHICAL AREA ARE ON THE BACK COVER OF YOUR TEST BOOKLET.
USE ONLY A NO. 2 OR HB PENCIL TO COMPLETE THIS ANSWER SHEET. DO NOT USE INK.

1 LAST NAME / FIRST NAME / MI

(Grid of bubbles A–Z for each letter position)

2 DATE OF BIRTH

MONTH	DAY	YEAR
○ Jan		
○ Feb		
○ Mar	0 0	0 0
○ Apr	1 1	1 1
○ May	2 2	2 2
○ June	3 3	3 3
○ July	4	4 4
○ Aug	5	5 5
○ Sept	6 6	6 6
○ Oct	7 7	7 7
○ Nov	8 8	8 8
○ Dec	9 9	9 9

3 SOCIAL SECURITY NO.

(Grid of bubbles 0–9)

Right Mark: ⬤

Wrong Marks: ⊘ Ⓧ ⊙

4 ETHNIC DESCRIPTION

- ○ American Indian/ Alaskan Native
- ○ Asian/Pacific Islander
- ○ Black/African Amer.
- ○ Canadian Aboriginal
- ○ Caucasian/White
- ○ Chicano/Mex. Amer.
- ○ Hispanic
- ○ Puerto Rican
- ○ Other

5 GENDER
- ○ Male
- ○ Female

6 DOMINANT LANGUAGE
- ○ English
- ○ Other

7 ENGLISH FLUENCY
- ○ Yes
- ○ No

8 CENTER NUMBER

(Grid of bubbles 0–9)

9 TEST FORM CODE

(Grid of bubbles 0–9)

10 TEST BOOK SERIAL NO.

11 TEST FORM

12 TEST DATE

_____ / _____ / _____
MONTH   DAY   YEAR

13 PLEASE PRINT ALL INFORMATION

LAST NAME   FIRST

MAILING ADDRESS

_____

_____

SOCIAL SECURITY/ SOCIAL INSURANCE NO.

LAW SCHOOL ADMISSION TEST

MARK ONE AND ONLY ONE ANSWER TO EACH QUESTION. BE SURE TO FILL IN COMPLETELY THE SPACE FOR YOUR INTENDED ANSWER CHOICE. IF YOU ERASE, DO SO COMPLETELY. MAKE NO STRAY MARKS.

SECTION 1 (Questions 1–30, each with options A B C D E)

SECTION 2 (Questions 1–30, each with options A B C D E)

SECTION 3 (Questions 1–30, each with options A B C D E)

SECTION 4 (Questions 1–30, each with options A B C D E)

SECTION 5 (Questions 1–30, each with options A B C D E)

NOTE: If you have a new address, you must write Law Services at Box 2000-C, Newtown, PA 18940 or call (215) 968-1001. We cannot guarantee that all address changes will be processed before scores are mailed, so be sure to notify your post office of your forwarding address.

FOR LAW SERVICES USE ONLY

LR	
LW	
LCS	

SECTION I
Time—35 minutes
28 Questions

Directions: Each passage in this section is followed by a group of questions to be answered on the basis of what is <u>stated</u> or <u>implied</u> in the passage. For some of the questions, more than one of the choices could conceivably answer the question. However, you are to choose the <u>best</u> answer; that is, the response that most accurately and completely answers the question, and blacken the corresponding space on your answer sheet.

There is substantial evidence that by 1926, with the publication of *The Weary Blues*, Langston Hughes had broken with two well-established traditions in African American literature. In *The*
(5) *Weary Blues*, Hughes chose to modify the traditions that decreed that African American literature must promote racial acceptance and integration, and that, in order to do so, it must reflect an understanding and mastery of Western European literary
(10) techniques and styles. Necessarily excluded by this decree, linguistically and thematically, was the vast amount of secular folk material in the oral tradition that had been created by Black people in the years of slavery and after. It might be pointed out that even
(15) the spirituals or "sorrow songs" of the slaves—as distinct from their secular songs and stories—had been Europeanized to make them acceptable within these African American traditions after the Civil War. In 1862 northern White writers had
(20) commented favorably on the unique and provocative melodies of these "sorrow songs" when they first heard them sung by slaves in the Carolina sea islands. But by 1916, ten years before the publication of *The Weary Blues*, Harry T. Burleigh, the Black
(25) baritone soloist at New York's ultrafashionable Saint George's Episcopal Church, had published *Jubilee Songs of the United States*, with every spiritual arranged so that a concert singer could sing it "in the manner of an art song." Clearly, the artistic work of
(30) Black people could be used to promote racial acceptance and integration only on the condition that it became Europeanized.

Even more than his rebellion against this restrictive tradition in African American art,
(35) Hughes's expression of the vibrant folk culture of Black people established his writing as a landmark in the history of African American literature. Most of his folk poems have the distinctive marks of this folk culture's oral tradition: they contain many instances
(40) of naming and enumeration, considerable hyperbole and understatement, and a strong infusion of street-talk rhyming. There is a deceptive veil of artlessness in these poems. Hughes prided himself on being an impromptu and impressionistic writer of
(45) poetry. His, he insisted, was not an artfully constructed poetry. Yet an analysis of his dramatic monologues and other poems reveals that his poetry was carefully and artfully crafted. In his folk poetry we find features common to all folk literature, such
(50) as dramatic ellipsis, narrative compression, rhythmic repetition, and monosyllabic emphasis. The peculiar mixture of irony and humor we find in his writing is a distinguishing feature of his folk poetry. Together, these aspects of Hughes's writing helped to modify
(55) the previous restrictions on the techniques and subject matter of Black writers and consequently to broaden the linguistic and thematic range of African American literature.

1. The author mentions which one of the following as an example of the influence of Black folk culture on Hughes's poetry?

(A) his exploitation of ambiguous and deceptive meanings
(B) his care and craft in composing poems
(C) his use of naming and enumeration
(D) his use of first-person narrative
(E) his strong religious beliefs

2. The author suggests that the "deceptive veil" (line 42) in Hughes's poetry obscures

(A) evidence of his use of oral techniques in his poetry
(B) evidence of his thoughtful deliberation in composing his poems
(C) his scrupulous concern for representative details in his poetry
(D) his incorporation of Western European literary techniques in his poetry
(E) his engagement with social and political issues rather than aesthetic ones

3. With which one of the following statements regarding *Jubilee Songs of the United States* would the author be most likely to agree?

(A) Its publication marked an advance in the intrinsic quality of African American art.
(B) It paved the way for publication of Hughes's *The Weary Blues* by making African American art fashionable.
(C) It was an authentic replication of African American spirituals and "sorrow songs."
(D) It demonstrated the extent to which spirituals were adapted in order to make them more broadly accepted.
(E) It was to the spiritual what Hughes's *The Weary Blues* was to secular songs and stories.

GO ON TO THE NEXT PAGE

4. The author most probably mentions the reactions of northern White writers to non-Europeanized "sorrow songs" in order to

(A) indicate that modes of expression acceptable in the context of slavery in the South were acceptable only to a small number of White writers in the North after the Civil War

(B) contrast White writers' earlier appreciation of these songs with the growing tendency after the Civil War to regard Europeanized versions of the songs as more acceptable

(C) show that the requirement that such songs be Europeanized was internal to the African American tradition and was unrelated to the literary standards or attitudes of White writers

(D) demonstrate that such songs in their non-Europeanized form were more imaginative than Europeanized versions of the same songs

(E) suggest that White writers benefited more from exposure to African American art forms than Black writers did from exposure to European art forms

5. The passage suggests that the author would be most likely to agree with which one of the following statements about the requirement that Black writers employ Western European literary techniques?

(A) The requirement was imposed more for social than for aesthetic reasons.

(B) The requirement was a relatively unimportant aspect of the African American tradition.

(C) The requirement was the chief reason for Hughes's success as a writer.

(D) The requirement was appropriate for some forms of expression but not for others.

(E) The requirement was never as strong as it may have appeared to be.

6. Which one of the following aspects of Hughes's poetry does the author appear to value most highly?

(A) its novelty compared to other works of African American literature

(B) its subtle understatement compared to that of other kinds of folk literature

(C) its virtuosity in adapting musical forms to language

(D) its expression of the folk culture of Black people

(E) its universality of appeal achieved through the adoption of colloquial expressions

GO ON TO THE NEXT PAGE.

Historians generally agree that, of the great
modern innovations, the railroad had the most
far-reaching impact on major events in the United
States in the nineteenth and early twentieth
(5)   centuries, particularly on the Industrial Revolution.
There is, however, considerable disagreement among
cultural historians regarding public attitudes toward
the railroad, both at its inception in the 1830s and
during the half century between 1880 and 1930,
(10) when the national rail system was completed and
reached the zenith of its popularity in the United
States. In a recent book, John Stilgoe has addressed
this issue by arguing that the "romantic-era distrust"
of the railroad that he claims was present during the
(15) 1830s vanished in the decades after 1880. But the
argument he provides in support of this position is
unconvincing.
    What Stilgoe calls "romantic-era distrust" was in
fact the reaction of a minority of writers, artists, and
(20) intellectuals who distrusted the railroad not so much
for what it was as for what it signified. Thoreau and
Hawthorne appreciated, even admired, an improved
means of moving things and people from one place to
another. What these writers and others were
(25) concerned about was not the new machinery as such,
but the new kind of economy, social order, and
culture that it prefigured. In addition, Stilgoe is
wrong to imply that the critical attitude of these
writers was typical of the period; their distrust was
(30) largely a reaction against the prevailing attitude in
the 1830s that the railroad was an unqualified
improvement.
    Stilgoe's assertion that the ambivalence toward
the railroad exhibited by writers like Hawthorne and
(35) Thoreau disappeared after the 1880s is also
misleading. In support of this thesis, Stilgoe has
unearthed an impressive volume of material, the
work of hitherto unknown illustrators, journalists,
and novelists, all devotees of the railroad; but it is not
(40) clear what this new material proves except perhaps
that the works of popular culture greatly expanded at
the time. The volume of the material proves nothing
if Stilgoe's point is that the earlier distrust of a
minority of intellectuals did not endure beyond the
(45) 1880s, and, oddly, much of Stilgoe's other evidence
indicates that it did. When he glances at the
treatment of railroads by writers like Henry James,
Sinclair Lewis, or F. Scott Fitzgerald, what comes
through in spite of Stilgoe's analysis is remarkably
(50) like Thoreau's feeling of contrariety and
ambivalence. (Had he looked at the work of Frank
Norris, Eugene O'Neill, or Henry Adams, Stilgoe's
case would have been much stronger.) The point is
that the sharp contrast between the enthusiastic
(55) supporters of the railroad in the 1830s and the
minority of intellectual dissenters during that period
extended into the 1880s and beyond.

7. The passage provides information to answer all of the
following questions EXCEPT:

(A) During what period did the railroad reach the
     zenith of its popularity in the United States?
(B) How extensive was the impact of the railroad on
     the Industrial Revolution in the United States,
     relative to that of other modern innovations?
(C) Who are some of the writers of the 1830s who
     expressed ambivalence toward the railroad?
(D) In what way could Stilgoe have strengthened
     his argument regarding intellectuals' attitudes
     toward the railroad in the years after the
     1880s?
(E) What arguments did the writers after the
     1880s, as cited by Stilgoe, offer to justify their
     support for the railroad?

8. According to the author of the passage, Stilgoe uses
the phrase "romantic-era distrust" (line 13) to imply
that the view he is referring to was

(A) the attitude of a minority of intellectuals toward
     technological innovation that began after 1830
(B) a commonly held attitude toward the railroad
     during the 1830s
(C) an ambivalent view of the railroad expressed by
     many poets and novelists between 1880 and
     1930
(D) a critique of social and economic developments
     during the 1830s by a minority of intellectuals
(E) an attitude toward the railroad that was
     disseminated by works of popular culture after
     1880

9. According to the author, the attitude toward the
railroad that was reflected in writings of Henry James,
Sinclair Lewis, and F. Scott Fitzgerald was

(A) influenced by the writings of Frank Norris,
     Eugene O'Neill, and Henry Adams
(B) similar to that of the minority of writers who
     had expressed ambivalence toward the railroad
     prior to the 1880s
(C) consistent with the public attitudes toward the
     railroad that were reflected in works of popular
     culture after the 1880s
(D) largely a reaction to the works of writers who
     had been severely critical of the railroad in the
     1830s
(E) consistent with the prevailing attitude toward
     the railroad during the 1830s

GO ON TO THE NEXT PAGE.

10. It can be inferred from the passage that the author uses the phrase "works of popular culture" (line 41) primarily to refer to the

(A) work of a large group of writers that was published between 1880 and 1930 and that in Stilgoe's view was highly critical of the railroad

(B) work of writers who were heavily influenced by Hawthorne and Thoreau

(C) large volume of writing produced by Henry Adams, Sinclair Lewis, and Eugene O'Neill

(D) work of journalists, novelists, and illustrators who were responsible for creating enthusiasm for the railroad during the 1830s

(E) work of journalists, novelists, and illustrators that was published after 1880 and that has received little attention from scholars other than Stilgoe

11. Which one of the following can be inferred from the passage regarding the work of Frank Norris, Eugene O'Neill, and Henry Adams?

(A) Their work never achieved broad popular appeal.

(B) Their ideas were disseminated to a large audience by the popular culture of the early 1800s.

(C) Their work expressed a more positive attitude toward the railroad than did that of Henry James, Sinclair Lewis, and F. Scott Fitzgerald.

(D) Although they were primarily novelists, some of their work could be classified as journalism.

(E) Although they were influenced by Thoreau, their attitude toward the railroad was significantly different from his.

12. It can be inferred from the passage that Stilgoe would be most likely to agree with which one of the following statements regarding the study of cultural history?

(A) It is impossible to know exactly what period historians are referring to when they use the term "romantic era."

(B) The writing of intellectuals often anticipates ideas and movements that are later embraced by popular culture.

(C) Writers who were not popular in their own time tell us little about the age in which they lived.

(D) The works of popular culture can serve as a reliable indicator of public attitudes toward modern innovations like the railroad.

(E) The best source of information concerning the impact of an event as large as the Industrial Revolution is the private letters and journals of individuals.

13. The primary purpose of the passage is to

(A) evaluate one scholar's view of public attitudes toward the railroad in the United States from the early nineteenth to the early twentieth century

(B) review the treatment of the railroad in American literature of the nineteenth and twentieth centuries

(C) survey the views of cultural historians regarding the railroad's impact on major events in United States history

(D) explore the origins of the public support for the railroad that existed after the completion of a national rail system in the United States

(E) define what historians mean when they refer to the "romantic-era distrust" of the railroad

GO ON TO THE NEXT PAGE.

Three basic adaptive responses—regulatory, acclimatory, and developmental—may occur in organisms as they react to changing environmental conditions. In all three, adjustment of biological
(5) features (morphological adjustment) or of their use (functional adjustment) may occur. Regulatory responses involve rapid changes in the organism's use of its physiological apparatus—increasing or decreasing the rates of various processes, for
(10) example. Acclimation involves morphological change—thickening of fur or red blood cell proliferation—which alters physiology itself. Such structural changes require more time than regulatory response changes. Regulatory and acclimatory
(15) responses are both reversible.

Developmental responses, however, are usually permanent and irreversible; they become fixed in the course of the individual's development in response to environmental conditions at the time the response
(20) occurs. One such response occurs in many kinds of water bugs. Most water-bug species inhabiting small lakes and ponds have two generations per year. The first hatches during the spring, reproduces during the summer, then dies. The eggs laid in the summer
(25) hatch and develop into adults in late summer. They live over the winter before breeding in early spring. Individuals in the second (overwintering) generation have fully developed wings and leave the water in autumn to overwinter in forests, returning in spring
(30) to small bodies of water to lay eggs. Their wings are absolutely necessary for this seasonal dispersal. The summer (early) generation, in contrast, is usually dimorphic—some individuals have normal functional (macropterous) wings; others have much-reduced
(35) (micropterous) wings of no use for flight. The summer generation's dimorphism is a compromise strategy, for these individuals usually do not leave the ponds and thus generally have no use for fully developed wings. But small ponds occasionally dry up
(40) during the summer, forcing the water bugs to search for new habitats, an eventuality that macropterous individuals are well adapted to meet.

The dimorphism of micropterous and macropterous individuals in the summer generation
(45) expresses developmental flexibility; it is not genetically determined. The individual's wing form is environmentally determined by the temperature to which developing eggs are exposed prior to their being laid. Eggs maintained in a warm environment
(50) always produce bugs with normal wings, but exposure to cold produces micropterous individuals. Eggs producing the overwintering brood are all formed during the late summer's warm temperatures. Hence, all individuals in the

(55) overwintering brood have normal wings. Eggs laid by the overwintering adults in the spring, which develop into the summer generation of adults, are formed in early autumn and early spring. Those eggs formed in autumn are exposed to cold winter temperatures, and
(60) thus produce micropterous adults in the summer generation. Those formed during the spring are never exposed to cold temperatures, and thus yield individuals with normal wings. Adult water bugs of the overwintering generation, brought into the
(65) laboratory during the cold months and kept warm, produce only macropterous offspring.

14. The primary purpose of the passage is to

(A) illustrate an organism's functional adaptive response to changing environmental conditions
(B) prove that organisms can exhibit three basic adaptive responses to changing environmental conditions
(C) explain the differences in form and function between micropterous and macropterous water bugs and analyze the effect of environmental changes on each
(D) discuss three different types of adaptive responses and provide an example that explains how one of those types of responses works
(E) contrast acclimatory responses with developmental responses and suggest an explanation for the evolutionary purposes of these two responses to changing environmental conditions

15. The passage supplies information to suggest that which one of the following would happen if a pond inhabited by water bugs were to dry up in June?

(A) The number of developmental responses among the water-bug population would decrease.
(B) Both micropterous and macropterous water bugs would show an acclimatory response.
(C) The generation of water bugs to be hatched during the subsequent spring would contain an unusually large number of macropterous individuals.
(D) The dimorphism of the summer generation would enable some individuals to survive.
(E) The dimorphism of the summer generation would be genetically transferred to the next spring generation.

GO ON TO THE NEXT PAGE.

16. It can be inferred from the passage that if the winter months of a particular year were unusually warm, the

(A) eggs formed by water bugs in the autumn would probably produce a higher than usual proportion of macropterous individuals

(B) eggs formed by water bugs in the autumn would probably produce an entire summer generation of water bugs with smaller than normal wings

(C) eggs of the overwintering generation formed in the autumn would not be affected by this temperature change

(D) overwintering generation would not leave the ponds for the forest during the winter

(E) overwintering generation of water bugs would most likely form fewer eggs in the autumn and more in the spring

17. According to the passage, the dimorphic wing structure of the summer generation of water bugs occurs because

(A) the overwintering generation forms two sets of eggs, one exposed to the colder temperatures of winter and one exposed only to the warmer temperatures of spring

(B) the eggs that produce micropterous and macropterous adults are morphologically different

(C) water bugs respond to seasonal changes by making an acclimatory functional adjustment in the wings

(D) water bugs hatching in the spring live out their life spans in ponds and never need to fly

(E) the overwintering generation, which produces eggs developing into the dimorphic generation, spends the winter in the forest and the spring in small ponds

18. It can be inferred from the passage that which one of the following is an example of a regulatory response?

(A) thickening of the plumage of some birds in the autumn

(B) increase in pulse rate during vigorous exercise

(C) gradual darkening of the skin after exposure to sunlight

(D) gradual enlargement of muscles as a result of weight lifting

(E) development of a heavy fat layer in bears before hibernation

19. According to the passage, the generation of water bugs hatching during the summer is likely to

(A) be made up of equal numbers of macropterous and micropterous individuals

(B) lay its eggs during the winter in order to expose them to cold

(C) show a marked inability to fly from one pond to another

(D) exhibit genetically determined differences in wing form from the early spring-hatched generation

(E) contain a much greater proportion of macropterous water bugs than the early spring-hatched generation

20. The author mentions laboratory experiments with adult water bugs (lines 63–66) in order to illustrate which one of the following?

(A) the function of the summer generation's dimorphism

(B) the irreversibility of most developmental adaptive responses in water bugs

(C) the effect of temperature on developing water-bug eggs

(D) the morphological difference between the summer generation and the overwintering generation of water bugs

(E) the functional adjustment of water bugs in response to seasonal temperature variation

21. Which one of the following best describes the organization of the passage?

(A) Biological phenomena are presented, examples of their occurrence are compared and contrasted, and one particular example is illustrated in detail.

(B) A description of related biological phenomena is stated, and two of those phenomena are explained in detail with illustrated examples.

(C) Three related biological phenomena are described, a hypothesis explaining their relationship is presented, and supporting evidence is produced.

(D) Three complementary biological phenomena are explained, their causes are examined, and one of them is described by contrasting its causes with the other two.

(E) A new way of describing biological phenomena is suggested, its applications are presented, and one specific example is examined in detail.

GO ON TO THE NEXT PAGE.

The Constitution of the United States does not explicitly define the extent of the President's authority to involve United States troops in conflicts with other nations in the absence of a declaration of
(5) war. Instead, the question of the President's authority in this matter falls in the hazy area of concurrent power, where authority is not expressly allocated to either the President or the Congress. The Constitution gives Congress the basic power to
(10) declare war, as well as the authority to raise and support armies and a navy, enact regulations for the control of the military, and provide for the common defense. The President, on the other hand, in addition to being obligated to execute the laws of the
(15) land, including commitments negotiated by defense treaties, is named commander in chief of the armed forces and is empowered to appoint envoys and make treaties with the consent of the Senate. Although this allocation of powers does not expressly address the
(20) use of armed forces short of a declared war, the spirit of the Constitution at least requires that Congress should be involved in the decision to deploy troops, and in passing the War Powers Resolution of 1973, Congress has at last reclaimed a role in such
(25) decisions.

Historically, United States Presidents have not waited for the approval of Congress before involving United States troops in conflicts in which a state of war was not declared. One scholar has identified 199
(30) military engagements that occurred without the consent of Congress, ranging from Jefferson's conflict with the Barbary pirates to Nixon's invasion of Cambodia during the Vietnam conflict, which President Nixon argued was justified because his role
(35) as commander in chief allowed him almost unlimited discretion over the deployment of troops. However, the Vietnam conflict, never a declared war, represented a turning point in Congress's tolerance of presidential discretion in the deployment of troops in
(40) undeclared wars. Galvanized by the human and monetary cost of those hostilities and showing a new determination to fulfill its proper role, Congress enacted the War Powers Resolution of 1973, a statute designed to ensure that the collective
(45) judgment of both Congress and the President would be applied to the involvement of United States troops in foreign conflicts.

The resolution required the President, in the absence of a declaration of war, to consult with
(50) Congress "in every possible instance" before introducing forces and to report to Congress within 48 hours after the forces have actually been deployed. Most important, the resolution allows Congress to veto the involvement once it begins, and
(55) requires the President, in most cases, to end the involvement within 60 days unless Congress specifically authorizes the military operation to continue. In its final section, by declaring that the resolution is not intended to alter the constitutional
(60) authority of either Congress or the President, the resolution asserts that congressional involvement in decisions to use armed force is in accord with the intent and spirit of the Constitution.

22. In the passage, the author is primarily concerned with

(A) showing how the Vietnam conflict led to a new interpretation of the Constitution's provisions for use of the military
(B) arguing that the War Powers Resolution of 1973 is an attempt to reclaim a share of constitutionally concurrent power that had been usurped by the President
(C) outlining the history of the struggle between the President and Congress for control of the military
(D) providing examples of conflicts inherent in the Constitution's approach to a balance of powers
(E) explaining how the War Powers Resolution of 1973 alters the Constitution to eliminate an overlap of authority

23. With regard to the use of United States troops in a foreign conflict without a formal declaration of war by the United States, the author believes that the United States Constitution does which one of the following?

(A) assumes that the President and Congress will agree on whether troops should be used
(B) provides a clear-cut division of authority between the President and Congress in the decision to use troops
(C) assigns a greater role to the Congress than to the President in deciding whether troops should be used
(D) grants final authority to the President to decide whether to use troops
(E) intends that both the President and Congress should be involved in the decision to use troops

GO ON TO THE NEXT PAGE.

24. The passage suggests that each of the following contributed to Congress's enacting the War Powers Resolution of 1973 EXCEPT

    (A) a change in the attitude in Congress toward exercising its role in the use of armed forces
    (B) the failure of Presidents to uphold commitments specified in defense treaties
    (C) Congress's desire to be consulted concerning United States military actions instigated by the President
    (D) the amount of money spent on recent conflicts waged without a declaration of war
    (E) the number of lives lost in Vietnam

25. It can be inferred from the passage that the War Powers Resolution of 1973 is applicable only in "the absence of a declaration of war" (lines 48–49) because

    (A) Congress has enacted other laws that already set out presidential requirements for situations in which war has been declared
    (B) by virtue of declaring war, Congress already implicitly participates in the decision to deploy troops
    (C) the President generally receives broad public support during wars that have been formally declared by Congress
    (D) Congress felt that the President should be allowed unlimited discretion in cases in which war has been declared
    (E) the United States Constitution already explicitly defines the reporting and consulting requirements of the President in cases in which war has been declared

26. It can be inferred from the passage that the author believes that the War Powers Resolution of 1973

    (A) is not in accord with the explicit roles of the President and Congress as defined in the Constitution
    (B) interferes with the role of the President as commander in chief of the armed forces
    (C) signals Congress's commitment to fulfill a role intended for it by the Constitution
    (D) fails explicitly to address the use of armed forces in the absence of a declaration of war
    (E) confirms the role historically assumed by Presidents

27. It can be inferred from the passage that the author would be most likely to agree with which one of the following statements regarding the invasion of Cambodia?

    (A) Because it was undertaken without the consent of Congress, it violated the intent and spirit of the Constitution.
    (B) Because it galvanized support for the War Powers Resolution, it contributed indirectly to the expansion of presidential authority.
    (C) Because it was necessitated by a defense treaty, it required the consent of Congress.
    (D) It served as a precedent for a new interpretation of the constitutional limits on the President's authority to deploy troops.
    (E) It differed from the actions of past Presidents in deploying United States troops in conflicts without a declaration of war by Congress.

28. According to the provisions of the War Powers Resolution of 1973 as described in the passage, if the President perceives that an international conflict warrants the immediate involvement of United States armed forces, the President is compelled in every instance to

    (A) request that Congress consider a formal declaration of war
    (B) consult with the leaders of both houses of Congress before deploying armed forces
    (C) desist from deploying any troops unless expressly approved by Congress
    (D) report to Congress within 48 hours of the deployment of armed forces
    (E) withdraw any armed forces deployed in such a conflict within 60 days unless war is declared

S T O P

IF YOU FINISH BEFORE TIME IS CALLED, YOU MAY CHECK YOUR WORK ON THIS SECTION ONLY.
DO NOT WORK ON ANY OTHER SECTION IN THE TEST.

SECTION II

Time—35 minutes

24 Questions

Directions: The questions in this section are based on the reasoning contained in brief statements or passages. For some questions, more than one of the choices could conceivably answer the question. However, you are to choose the best answer; that is, the response that most accurately and completely answers the question. You should not make assumptions that are by commonsense standards implausible, superfluous, or incompatible with the passage. After you have chosen the best answer, blacken the corresponding space on your answer sheet.

1. Some people believe that witnessing violence in movies will discharge aggressive energy. Does watching someone else eat fill one's own stomach?

   In which one of the following does the reasoning most closely parallel that employed in the passage?

   (A) Some people think appropriating supplies at work for their own personal use is morally wrong. Isn't shoplifting morally wrong?
   (B) Some people think nationalism is defensible. Hasn't nationalism been the excuse for committing abominable crimes?
   (C) Some people think that boxing is fixed just because wrestling usually is. Are the two sports managed by the same sort of people?
   (D) Some people think that economists can control inflation. Can meteorologists make the sun shine?
   (E) Some people think workaholics are compensating for a lack of interpersonal skills. However, aren't most doctors workaholics?

2. Ann: All the campers at Camp Winnehatchee go to Tri-Cities High School.
   Bill: That's not true. Some Tri-Cities students are campers at Camp Lakemont.

   Bill's answer can be best explained on the assumption that he has interpreted Ann's remark to mean that

   (A) most of the campers at Camp Lakemont come from high schools other than Tri-Cities
   (B) most Tri-Cities High School students are campers at Camp Winnehatchee
   (C) some Tri-Cities High School students have withdrawn from Camp Lakemont
   (D) all Tri-Cities High School students attend summer camp
   (E) only campers at Camp Winnehatchee are students at Tri-Cities High School

3. More than a year ago, the city announced that police would crack down on illegally parked cars and that resources would be diverted from writing speeding tickets to ticketing illegally parked cars. But no crackdown has taken place. The police chief claims that resources have had to be diverted from writing speeding tickets to combating the city's staggering drug problem. Yet the police are still writing as many speeding tickets as ever. Therefore, the excuse about resources being tied up in fighting drug-related crime simply is not true.

   The conclusion in the passage depends on the assumption that

   (A) every member of the police force is qualified to work on combating the city's drug problem
   (B) drug-related crime is not as serious a problem for the city as the police chief claims it is
   (C) writing speeding tickets should be as important a priority for the city as combating drug-related crime
   (D) the police could be cracking down on illegally parked cars and combating the drug problem without having to reduce writing speeding tickets
   (E) the police cannot continue writing as many speeding tickets as ever while diverting resources to combating drug-related crime

GO ON TO THE NEXT PAGE.

4. Dried grass clippings mixed into garden soil gradually decompose, providing nutrients for beneficial soil bacteria. This results in better-than-average plant growth. Yet mixing fresh grass clippings into garden soil usually causes poorer-than-average plant growth.

Which one of the following, if true, most helps to explain the difference in plant growth described above?

(A) The number of beneficial soil bacteria increases whenever any kind of plant material is mixed into garden soil.

(B) Nutrients released by dried grass clippings are immediately available to beneficial soil bacteria.

(C) Some dried grass clippings retain nutrients originally derived from commercial lawn fertilizers, and thus provide additional enrichment to the soil.

(D) Fresh grass clippings mixed into soil decompose rapidly, generating high levels of heat that kill beneficial soil bacteria.

(E) When a mix of fresh and dried grass clippings is mixed into garden soil, plant growth often decreases.

5. A gas tax of one cent per gallon would raise one billion dollars per year at current consumption rates. Since a tax of fifty cents per gallon would therefore raise fifty billion dollars per year, it seems a perfect way to deal with the federal budget deficit. This tax would have the additional advantage that the resulting drop in the demand for gasoline would be ecologically sound and would keep our country from being too dependent on foreign oil producers.

Which one of the following most clearly identifies an error in the author's reasoning?

(A) The author cites irrelevant data.

(B) The author relies on incorrect current consumption figures.

(C) The author makes incompatible assumptions.

(D) The author mistakes an effect for a cause.

(E) The author appeals to conscience rather than reason.

6. As symbols of the freedom of the wilderness, bald eagles have the unique capacity to inspire people and foster in them a sympathetic attitude toward the needs of other threatened species. Clearly, without that sympathy and the political will it engenders, the needs of more obscure species will go unmet. The conservation needs of many obscure species can only be met by beginning with the conservation of this symbolic species, the bald eagle.

Which one of the following is the main point of the passage as a whole?

(A) Because bald eagles symbolize freedom, conservation efforts should be concentrated on them rather than on other, more obscure species.

(B) The conservation of bald eagles is the first necessary step in conserving other endangered species.

(C) Without increased public sympathy for conservation, the needs of many symbolic species will go unmet.

(D) People's love of the wilderness can be used to engender political support for conservation efforts.

(E) Other threatened species do not inspire people or foster sympathy as much as do bald eagles.

7. There is no reason why the work of scientists has to be officially confirmed before being published. There is a system in place for the confirmation or disconfirmation of scientific findings, namely, the replication of results by other scientists. Poor scientific work on the part of any one scientist, which can include anything from careless reporting practices to fraud, is not harmful. It will be exposed and rendered harmless when other scientists conduct the experiments and obtain disconfirmatory results.

Which one of the following, if true, would weaken the argument?

(A) Scientific experiments can go unchallenged for many years before they are replicated.

(B) Most scientists work in universities, where their work is submitted to peer review before publication.

(C) Most scientists are under pressure to make their work accessible to the scrutiny of replication.

(D) In scientific experiments, careless reporting is more common than fraud.

(E) Most scientists work as part of a team rather than alone.

GO ON TO THE NEXT PAGE.

8. Alice: Quotas on automobile imports to the United States should be eliminated. Then domestic producers would have to compete directly with Japanese manufacturers and would be forced to produce higher-quality cars. Such competition would be good for consumers.

    David: You fail to realize, Alice, that quotas on automobile imports are pervasive worldwide. Since Germany, Britain, and France have quotas, so should the United States.

    Which one of the following most accurately characterizes David's response to Alice's statement?

    (A) David falsely accuses Alice of contradicting herself.
    (B) David unfairly directs his argument against Alice personally.
    (C) David uncovers a hidden assumption underlying Alice's position.
    (D) David takes a position that is similar to the one Alice has taken.
    (E) David fails to address the reasons Alice cites in favor of her conclusion.

9. Governments have only one response to public criticism of socially necessary services: regulation of the activity of providing those services. But governments inevitably make the activity more expensive by regulating it, and that is particularly troublesome in these times of strained financial resources. However, since public criticism of child-care services has undermined all confidence in such services, and since such services are socially necessary, the government is certain to respond.

    Which one of the following statements can be inferred from the passage?

    (A) The quality of child care will improve.
    (B) The cost of providing child-care services will increase.
    (C) The government will use funding to foster advances in child care.
    (D) If public criticism of policy is strongly voiced, the government is certain to respond.
    (E) If child-care services are not regulated, the cost of providing child care will not increase.

10. Advertisers are often criticized for their unscrupulous manipulation of people's tastes and wants. There is evidence, however, that some advertisers are motivated by moral as well as financial considerations. A particular publication decided to change its image from being a family newspaper to concentrating on sex and violence, thus appealing to a different readership. Some advertisers withdrew their advertisements from the publication, and this must have been because they morally disapproved of publishing salacious material.

    Which one of the following, if true, would most strengthen the argument?

    (A) The advertisers switched their advertisements to other family newspapers.
    (B) Some advertisers switched from family newspapers to advertise in the changed publication.
    (C) The advertisers expected their product sales to increase if they stayed with the changed publication, but to decrease if they withdrew.
    (D) People who generally read family newspapers are not likely to buy newspapers that concentrate on sex and violence.
    (E) It was expected that the changed publication would appeal principally to those in a different income group.

GO ON TO THE NEXT PAGE.

11. "If the forest continues to disappear at its present pace, the koala will approach extinction," said the biologist.

"So all that is needed to save the koala is to stop deforestation," said the politician.

Which one of the following statements is consistent with the biologist's claim but not with the politician's claim?

(A) Deforestation continues and the koala becomes extinct.
(B) Deforestation is stopped and the koala becomes extinct.
(C) Reforestation begins and the koala survives.
(D) Deforestation is slowed and the koala survives.
(E) Deforestation is slowed and the koala approaches extinction.

12. People have long been fascinated by the paranormal. Over the years, numerous researchers have investigated telepathy only to find that conclusive evidence for its existence has persistently evaded them. Despite this, there are still those who believe that there must be "something in it" since some research seems to support the view that telepathy exists. However, it can often be shown that other explanations that do comply with known laws can be given. Therefore, it is premature to conclude that telepathy is an alternative means of communication.

In the passage, the author

(A) supports the conclusion by pointing to the inadequacy of evidence for the opposite view
(B) supports the conclusion by describing particular experiments
(C) supports the conclusion by overgeneralizing from a specific piece of evidence
(D) draws a conclusion that is not supported by the premises
(E) rephrases the conclusion without offering any support for it

13. If retail stores experience a decrease in revenues during this holiday season, then either attitudes toward extravagant gift-giving have changed or prices have risen beyond the level most people can afford. If attitudes have changed, then we all have something to celebrate this season. If prices have risen beyond the level most people can afford, then it must be that salaries have not kept pace with rising prices during the past year.

Assume the premises above to be true. If salaries have kept pace with rising prices during the past year, which one of the following must be true?

(A) Attitudes toward extravagant gift-giving have changed.
(B) Retail stores will not experience a decrease in retail sales during this holiday season.
(C) Prices in retail stores have not risen beyond the level that most people can afford during this holiday season.
(D) Attitudes toward extravagant gift-giving have not changed, and stores will not experience a decrease in revenues during this holiday season.
(E) Either attitudes toward extravagant gift-giving have changed or prices have risen beyond the level that most people can afford during this holiday season.

GO ON TO THE NEXT PAGE.

14. The "suicide wave" that followed the United States stock market crash of October 1929 is more legend than fact. Careful examination of the monthly figures on the causes of death in 1929 shows that the number of suicides in October and in November was comparatively low. In only three other months were the monthly figures lower. During the summer months, when the stock market was flourishing, the number of suicides was substantially higher.

Which one of the following, if true, would best challenge the conclusion of the passage?

(A) The suicide rate is influenced by many psychological, interpersonal, and societal factors during any given historical period.
(B) October and November have almost always had relatively high suicide rates, even during the 1920s and 1930s.
(C) The suicide rate in October and November of 1929 was considerably higher than the average for those months during several preceding and following years.
(D) During the years surrounding the stock market crash, suicide rates were typically lower at the beginning of any calendar year than toward the end of that year.
(E) Because of seasonal differences, the number of suicides in October and November of 1929 would not be expected to be the same as those for other months.

15. A well-known sports figure found that combining publicity tours with playing tours led to problems, so she stopped combining the two. She no longer allows bookstore appearances and playing in competition to occur in the same city within the same trip. This week she is traveling to London to play in a major competition, so during her stay in London she will not be making any publicity appearances at any bookstore in London.

Which one of the following most closely parallels the reasoning used in the passage?

(A) Wherever there is an Acme Bugkiller, many wasps are killed. The Z family garden has an Acme Bugkiller, so any wasps remaining in the garden will soon be killed.
(B) The only times that the hospital's emergency room staff attends to relatively less serious emergencies are times when there is no critical emergency to attend to. On Monday night the emergency room staff attended to a series of fairly minor emergencies, so there must not have been any critical emergencies to take care of at the time.
(C) Tomato plants require hot summers to thrive. Farms in the cool summers of country Y probably do not have thriving tomato plants.
(D) Higher grades lead to better job opportunities, and studying leads to higher grades. Therefore, studying will lead to better job opportunities.
(E) Butter knives are not sharp. Q was not murdered with a sharp blade, so suspect X's butter knife may have been the murder weapon.

GO ON TO THE NEXT PAGE.

Questions 16–17

The advanced technology of ski boots and bindings has brought a dramatic drop in the incidence of injuries that occur on the slopes of ski resorts: from 9 injuries per 1,000 skiers in 1950 to 3 in 1980. As a result, the remainder of ski-related injuries, which includes all injuries occurring on the premises of a ski resort but not on the slopes, rose from 10 percent of all ski-related injuries in 1950 to 25 percent in 1980. The incidence of these injuries, including accidents such as falling down steps, increases with the amount of alcohol consumed per skier.

16. Which one of the following can be properly inferred from the passage?

   (A) As the number of ski injuries that occur on the slopes decreases, the number of injuries that occur on the premises of ski resorts increases.
   (B) The amount of alcohol consumed per skier increased between 1950 and 1980.
   (C) The technology of ski boots and bindings affects the incidence of each type of ski-related injury.
   (D) If the technology of ski boots and bindings continues to advance, the incidence of ski-related injuries will continue to decline.
   (E) Injuries that occurred on the slopes of ski resorts made up a smaller percentage of ski-related injuries in 1980 than in 1950.

17. Which one of the following conflicts with information in the passage?

   (A) The number of ski injuries that occurred on the slopes was greater in 1980 than in 1950.
   (B) A skier was less likely to be injured on the slopes in 1950 than in 1980.
   (C) The reporting of ski injuries became more accurate between 1950 and 1980.
   (D) The total number of skiers dropped between 1950 and 1980.
   (E) Some ski-related injuries occurred in 1980 to people who were not skiing.

18. Learning how to build a nest plays an important part in the breeding success of birds. For example, Dr. Snow has recorded the success of a number of blackbirds in several successive years. He finds that birds nesting for the first time are less successful in breeding than are older birds, and also less successful than they themselves are a year later. This cannot be a mere matter of size and strength, since blackbirds, like the great majority of birds, are fully grown when they leave the nest. It is difficult to avoid the conclusion that they benefit by their nesting experience.

Which one of the following, if true, would most weaken the argument?

   (A) Blackbirds build better nests than other birds.
   (B) The capacity of blackbirds to lay viable eggs increases with each successive trial during the first few years of reproduction.
   (C) The breeding success of birds nesting for the second time is greater than that of birds nesting for the first time.
   (D) Smaller and weaker blackbirds breed just as successfully as bigger and stronger blackbirds.
   (E) Up to 25 percent of all birds are killed by predators before they start to nest.

19. How do the airlines expect to prevent commercial plane crashes? Studies have shown that pilot error contributes to two-thirds of all such crashes. To address this problem, the airlines have upgraded their training programs by increasing the hours of classroom instruction and emphasizing communication skills in the cockpit. But it is unrealistic to expect such measures to compensate for pilots' lack of actual flying time. Therefore, the airlines should rethink their training approach to reducing commercial crashes.

Which one of the following is an assumption upon which the argument depends?

   (A) Training programs can eliminate pilot errors.
   (B) Commercial pilots routinely undergo additional training throughout their careers.
   (C) The number of airline crashes will decrease if pilot training programs focus on increasing actual flying time.
   (D) Lack of actual flying time is an important contributor to pilot error in commercial plane crashes.
   (E) Communication skills are not important to pilot training programs.

GO ON TO THE NEXT PAGE.

20. All savings accounts are interest-bearing accounts. The interest from some interest-bearing accounts is tax-free, so there must be some savings accounts that have tax-free interest.

Which one of the following arguments is flawed in a way most similar to the way in which the passage is flawed?

(A) All artists are intellectuals. Some great photographers are artists. Therefore, some great photographers must be intellectuals.

(B) All great photographers are artists. All artists are intellectuals. Therefore, some great photographers must be intellectuals.

(C) All great photographers are artists. Some artists are intellectuals. Therefore, some great photographers are intellectuals.

(D) All great photographers are artists. Some great photographers are intellectuals. Therefore, some artists must be intellectuals.

(E) All great photographers are artists. No artists are intellectuals. Therefore, some great photographers must not be intellectuals.

21. One method of dating the emergence of species is to compare the genetic material of related species. Scientists theorize that the more genetically similar two species are to each other, the more recently they diverged from a common ancestor. After comparing genetic material from giant pandas, red pandas, raccoons, coatis, and all seven bear species, scientists concluded that bears and raccoons diverged 30 to 50 million years ago. They further concluded that red pandas separated from the ancestor of today's raccoons and coatis a few million years later, some 10 million years before giant pandas diverged from the other bears.

Which one of the following can be properly inferred from the passage?

(A) Giant pandas and red pandas are more closely related than scientists originally thought they were.

(B) Scientists now count the giant panda as the eighth species of bear.

(C) It is possible to determine, within a margin of just a few years, the timing of divergence of various species.

(D) Scientists have found that giant pandas are more similar genetically to bears than to raccoons.

(E) There is substantial consensus among scientists that giant pandas and red pandas are equally related to raccoons.

GO ON TO THE NEXT PAGE.

Questions 22–23

Despite improvements in treatment for asthma, the death rate from this disease has doubled during the past decade from its previous rate. Two possible explanations for this increase have been offered. First, the recording of deaths due to asthma has become more widespread and accurate in the past decade than it had been previously. Second, there has been an increase in urban pollution. However, since the rate of deaths due to asthma has increased dramatically even in cities with long-standing, comprehensive medical records and with little or no urban pollution, one must instead conclude that the cause of increased deaths is the use of bronchial inhalers by asthma sufferers to relieve their symptoms.

22. Each of the following, if true, provides support to the argument EXCEPT:

   (A) Urban populations have doubled in the past decade.
   (B) Records of asthma deaths are as accurate for the past twenty years as for the past ten years.
   (C) Evidence suggests that bronchial inhalers make the lungs more sensitive to irritation by airborne pollen.
   (D) By temporarily relieving the symptoms of asthma, inhalers encourage sufferers to avoid more beneficial measures.
   (E) Ten years ago bronchial inhalers were not available as an asthma treatment.

23. Which one of the following is an assumption on which the argument depends?

   (A) Urban pollution has not doubled in the past decade.
   (B) Doctors and patients generally ignore the role of allergies in asthma.
   (C) Bronchial inhalers are unsafe, even when used according to the recommended instructions.
   (D) The use of bronchial inhalers aggravates other diseases that frequently occur among asthma sufferers and that often lead to fatal outcomes even when the asthma itself does not.
   (E) Increased urban pollution, improved recording of asthma deaths, and the use of bronchial inhalers are the only possible explanations of the increased death rate due to asthma.

24. There is little point in looking to artists for insights into political issues. Most of them hold political views that are less insightful than those of any reasonably well-educated person who is not an artist. Indeed, when taken as a whole, the statements made by artists, including those considered to be great, indicate that artistic talent and political insight are rarely found together.

Which one of the following can be inferred from the passage?

   (A) There are no artists who have insights into political issues.
   (B) A thorough education in art makes a person reasonably well educated.
   (C) Every reasonably well-educated person who is not an artist has more insight into political issues than any artist.
   (D) Politicians rarely have any artistic talent.
   (E) Some artists are no less politically insightful than some reasonably well-educated persons who are not artists.

S T O P

IF YOU FINISH BEFORE TIME IS CALLED, YOU MAY CHECK YOUR WORK ON THIS SECTION ONLY.
DO NOT WORK ON ANY OTHER SECTION IN THE TEST.

SECTION III

Time—35 minutes

24 Questions

Directions: Each group of questions in this section is based on a set of conditions. In answering some of the questions, it may be useful to draw a rough diagram. Choose the response that most accurately and completely answers each question and blacken the corresponding space on your answer sheet.

Questions 1–5

The Mammoth Corporation has just completed hiring nine new workers: Brandt, Calva, Duvall, Eberle, Fu, Garcia, Haga, Irving, and Jessup.

   Fu and Irving were hired on the same day as each other, and no one else was hired that day.
   Calva and Garcia were hired on the same day as each other, and no one else was hired that day.
   On each of the other days of hiring, exactly one worker was hired.
   Eberle was hired before Brandt.
   Haga was hired before Duvall.
   Duvall was hired after Irving but before Eberle.
   Garcia was hired after both Jessup and Brandt.
   Brandt was hired before Jessup.

1. Who were the last two workers to be hired?

    (A) Eberle and Jessup
    (B) Brandt and Garcia
    (C) Brandt and Calva
    (D) Garcia and Calva
    (E) Jessup and Brandt

2. Who was hired on the fourth day of hiring?

    (A) Eberle
    (B) Brandt
    (C) Irving
    (D) Garcia
    (E) Jessup

3. Exactly how many workers were hired before Jessup?

    (A) 6
    (B) 5
    (C) 4
    (D) 3
    (E) 2

4. Which one of the following must be true?

    (A) Duvall was the first worker to be hired.
    (B) Haga was the first worker to be hired.
    (C) Fu and Irving were the first two workers to be hired.
    (D) Haga and Fu were the first two workers to be hired.
    (E) Either Haga was the first worker to be hired or Fu and Irving were the first two workers to be hired.

5. If Eberle was hired on a Monday, what is the earliest day on which Garcia could have been hired?

    (A) Monday
    (B) Tuesday
    (C) Wednesday
    (D) Thursday
    (E) Friday

GO ON TO THE NEXT PAGE.

Questions 6–12

An apartment building has five floors. Each floor has either one or two apartments. There are exactly eight apartments in the building. The residents of the building are J, K, L, M, N, O, P, and Q, who each live in a different apartment.

J lives on a floor with two apartments.
K lives on the floor directly above P.
The second floor is made up of only one apartment.
M and N live on the same floor.
O does not live on the same floor as Q.
L lives in the only apartment on her floor.
Q does not live on the first or second floor.

6. Which one of the following must be true?

   (A)   Q lives on the third floor.
   (B)   Q lives on the fifth floor.
   (C)   L does not live on the fourth floor.
   (D)   N does not live on the second floor.
   (E)   J lives on the first floor.

7. Which one of the following CANNOT be true?

   (A)   K lives on the second floor.
   (B)   M lives on the first floor.
   (C)   N lives on the fourth floor.
   (D)   O lives on the third floor.
   (E)   P lives on the fifth floor.

8. If J lives on the fourth floor and K lives on the fifth floor, which one of the following can be true?

   (A)   O lives on the first floor.
   (B)   Q lives on the fourth floor.
   (C)   N lives on the fifth floor.
   (D)   L lives on the fourth floor.
   (E)   P lives on the third floor.

9. If O lives on the second floor, which one of the following CANNOT be true?

   (A)   K lives on the fourth floor.
   (B)   K lives on the fifth floor.
   (C)   L lives on the first floor.
   (D)   L lives on the third floor.
   (E)   L lives on the fourth floor.

10. If M lives on the fourth floor, which one of the following must be false?

    (A)   O lives on the fifth floor.
    (B)   J lives on the first floor.
    (C)   L lives on the second floor.
    (D)   Q lives on the third floor.
    (E)   P lives on the first floor.

11. Which one of the following must be true?

    (A)   If J lives on the fourth floor, then Q does not live on the fifth floor.
    (B)   If O lives on the second floor, then L does not live on the fourth floor.
    (C)   If N lives on the fourth floor, then K does not live on the second floor.
    (D)   If K lives on the third floor, then O does not live on the fifth floor.
    (E)   If P lives on the fourth floor, then M does not live on the third floor.

12. If O lives on the fourth floor and P lives on the second floor, which one of the following must be true?

    (A)   L lives on the first floor.
    (B)   M lives on the third floor.
    (C)   Q lives on the third floor.
    (D)   N lives on the fifth floor.
    (E)   Q lives on the fifth floor.

GO ON TO THE NEXT PAGE.

Questions 13–17

Hannah spends 14 days, exclusive of travel time, in a total of six cities.

Each city she visits is in one of three countries—X, Y, or Z.

Each of the three countries has many cities.

Hannah visits at least one city in each of the three countries.

She spends at least two days in each city she visits.

She spends only whole days in any city.

13. If Hannah spends exactly eight days in the cities of country X, then which one of the following CANNOT be true?

   (A)   She visits exactly two cities in country X.
   (B)   She visits exactly two cities in country Y.
   (C)   She visits exactly two cities in country Z.
   (D)   She visits more cities in country Y than in country Z.
   (E)   She visits more cities in country Z than in country Y.

14. If Hannah visits an equal number of cities in each of the countries, what is the greatest total number of days she can spend visiting cities in country X?

   (A)   3
   (B)   4
   (C)   5
   (D)   6
   (E)   7

15. If Hannah spends three days in the cities of country Y and seven days in the cities of country Z, then which one of the following must be false?

   (A)   She visits more cities in country X than in country Y.
   (B)   She visits exactly two cities in country X.
   (C)   She visits more cities in country Z than in country X.
   (D)   She visits exactly two cities in country Z.
   (E)   She visits exactly three cities in country Z.

16. If the city of Nomo is in country X, and if Hannah spends as many days as possible in Nomo and as few days as possible in each of the other cities that she visits, then which one of the following must be true?

   (A)   Hannah cannot visit any other cities in country X.
   (B)   Hannah can visit four cities in country Y.
   (C)   Hannah can spend six days in Nomo.
   (D)   Hannah cannot spend more than four days in country Z.
   (E)   Hannah can visit, at most, a total of four cities in countries Y and Z.

17. If Hannah visits a combined total of four cities in countries X and Y, what is the greatest total number of days she can spend visiting cities in country Y?

   (A)   6
   (B)   7
   (C)   8
   (D)   9
   (E)   10

GO ON TO THE NEXT PAGE.

Questions 18–24

Exactly six dogs—P, Q, R, S, T, and U—are entered in a dog show. The judge of the show awards exactly four ribbons, one for each of first, second, third, and fourth places, to four of the dogs. The information that follows is all that is available about the six dogs:

Each dog is either a greyhound or a labrador, but not both.

Two of the six dogs are female and four are male.

The judge awards ribbons to both female dogs, exactly one of which is a labrador.

Exactly one labrador wins a ribbon.

Dogs P and R place ahead of dog S, and dog S places ahead of dogs Q and T.

Dogs P and R are greyhounds.

Dogs S and U are labradors.

18. Which one of the following is a complete and accurate list of the dogs that can be greyhounds?

(A) P, Q
(B) P, R
(C) P, Q, R
(D) P, R, T
(E) P, Q, R, T

19. Which one of the following statements CANNOT be true?

(A) A female greyhound wins the second place ribbon.
(B) A female labrador wins the second place ribbon.
(C) A female labrador wins the third place ribbon.
(D) A male greyhound wins the fourth place ribbon.
(E) A female greyhound wins the fourth place ribbon.

20. Which one of the following dogs must be male?

(A) dog P
(B) dog R
(C) dog S
(D) dog T
(E) dog U

21. Which one of the following statements can be false?

(A) Dog P places ahead of dog R.
(B) Dog P places ahead of dog T.
(C) Dog R places ahead of dog U.
(D) Dog R places ahead of dog T.
(E) Dog S places ahead of dog U.

22. If dog Q is female, which one of the following statements can be false?

(A) Dog P is male.
(B) Dog R is male.
(C) Dog Q wins the fourth place ribbon.
(D) Dog Q is a greyhound.
(E) Dog T is a greyhound.

23. If dog T wins the fourth place ribbon, then which one of the following statements must be true?

(A) Dog P is male.
(B) Dog Q is male.
(C) Dog T is male.
(D) Dog Q is a labrador.
(E) Dog T is a labrador.

24. Which one of the following statements could be true?

(A) Dog P does not win a ribbon.
(B) Dog R does not win a ribbon.
(C) Dog S does not win a ribbon.
(D) Dog T wins a ribbon.
(E) Dog U wins a ribbon.

S T O P

IF YOU FINISH BEFORE TIME IS CALLED, YOU MAY CHECK YOUR WORK ON THIS SECTION ONLY.
DO NOT WORK ON ANY OTHER SECTION IN THE TEST.

SECTION IV

Time—35 minutes

25 Questions

Directions: The questions in this section are based on the reasoning contained in brief statements or passages. For some questions, more than one of the choices could conceivably answer the question. However, you are to choose the best answer; that is, the response that most accurately and completely answers the question. You should not make assumptions that are by commonsense standards implausible, superfluous, or incompatible with the passage. After you have chosen the best answer, blacken the corresponding space on your answer sheet.

1. A major art theft from a museum was remarkable in that the pieces stolen clearly had been carefully selected. The criterion for selection, however, clearly had not been greatest estimated market value. It follows that the theft was specifically carried out to suit the taste of some individual collector for whose private collection the pieces were destined.

    The argument tacitly appeals to which one of the following principles?

    (A) Any art theft can, on the evidence of the selection of pieces stolen, be categorized as committed either at the direction of a single known individual or at the direction of a group of known individuals.
    (B) Any art theft committed at the direction of a single individual results in a pattern of works taken and works left alone that defies rational analysis.
    (C) The pattern of works taken and works left alone can sometimes distinguish one type of art theft from another.
    (D) Art thefts committed with no preexisting plan for the disposition of the stolen works do not always involve theft of the most valuable pieces only.
    (E) The pattern of works taken and works left alone in an art theft can be particularly damaging to the integrity of the remaining collection.

2. The teeth of some mammals show "growth rings" that result from the constant depositing of layers of cementum as opaque bands in summer and translucent bands in winter. Cross sections of pigs' teeth found in an excavated Stone Age trash pit revealed bands of remarkably constant width except that the band deposited last, which was invariably translucent, was only about half the normal width.

    The statements above most strongly support the conclusion that the animals died

    (A) in an unusually early winter
    (B) at roughly the same age
    (C) roughly in midwinter
    (D) in a natural catastrophe
    (E) from starvation

3. The United States has never been a great international trader. It found most of its raw materials and customers for finished products within its own borders. The terrible consequences of this situation have become apparent, as this country now owes the largest foreign debt in the world and is a playground for wealthy foreign investors. The moral is clear: a country can no more live without foreign trade than a dog can live by eating its own tail.

    In order to advance her point of view, the author does each of the following EXCEPT

    (A) draw on an analogy
    (B) appeal to historical fact
    (C) identify a cause and an effect
    (D) suggest a cause of the current economic situation
    (E) question the ethical basis of an economic situation

GO ON TO THE NEXT PAGE.

4. Giselle: The government needs to ensure that the public consumes less petroleum. When things cost more, people buy and use less of them. Therefore, the government should raise the sales tax on gasoline, a major petroleum product.

   Antoine: The government should not raise the sales tax on gasoline. Such an increase would be unfair to gasoline users. If taxes are to be increased, the increases should be applied in such a way that they spread the burden of providing the government with increased revenues among many people, not just the users of gasoline.

As a rebuttal of Giselle's argument, Antoine's response is ineffective because

(A)   he ignores the fact that Giselle does not base her argument for raising the gasoline sales tax on the government's need for increased revenues

(B)   he fails to specify how many taxpayers there are who are not gasoline users

(C)   his conclusion is based on an assertion regarding unfairness, and unfairness is a very subjective concept

(D)   he mistakenly assumes that Giselle wants a sales tax increase only on gasoline

(E)   he makes the implausible assumption that the burden of increasing government revenues can be more evenly distributed among the people through other means besides increasing the gasoline sales tax

5. A government agency publishes ratings of airlines, ranking highest the airlines that have the smallest proportion of late flights. The agency's purpose is to establish an objective measure of the relative efficiency of different airlines' personnel in meeting published flight schedules.

Which one of the following, if true, would tend to invalidate use of the ratings for the agency's purpose?

(A)   Travelers sometimes have no choice of airlines for a given trip at a given time.

(B)   Flights are often made late by bad weather conditions that affect some airlines more than others.

(C)   The flight schedules of all airlines allow extra time for flights that go into or out of very busy airports.

(D)   Airline personnel are aware that the government agency is monitoring all airline flights for lateness.

(E)   Flights are defined as "late" only if they arrive more than fifteen minutes past their scheduled arrival time, and a record is made of how much later than fifteen minutes they are.

6. Although this bottle is labeled "vinegar," no fizzing occurred when some of the liquid in it was added to powder from this box labeled "baking soda." But when an acidic liquid such as vinegar is added to baking soda the resulting mixture fizzes, so this bottle clearly has been mislabeled.

A flaw in the reasoning in the argument above is that this argument

(A)   ignores the possibility that the bottle contained an acidic liquid other than vinegar

(B)   fails to exclude an alternative explanation for the observed effect

(C)   depends on the use of the imprecise term "fizz"

(D)   does not take into account the fact that scientific principles can be definitively tested only under controlled laboratory conditions

(E)   assumes that the fact of a labeling error is proof of an intention to deceive

GO ON TO THE NEXT PAGE.

7. Marine biologists have long thought that variation in the shell color of aquatic snails evolved as a protective camouflage against birds and other predators. Brown shells seem to be more frequent when the underlying seafloor is dark-colored and white shells more frequent when the underlying seafloor is light-colored. A new theory has been advanced, however, that claims that shell color is related to physiological stress associated with heat absorption. According to this theory, brown shells will be more prevalent in areas where the wave action of the sea is great and thus heat absorption from the Sun is minimized, whereas white shells will be more numerous in calmer waters where the snails will absorb more heat from the Sun's rays.

Evidence that would strongly favor the new theory over the traditional theory would be the discovery of a large majority of

(A) dark-shelled snails in a calm inlet with a dark, rocky bottom and many predators
(B) dark-shelled snails in a calm inlet with a white, sandy bottom
(C) light-shelled snails in an inlet with much wave action and a dark, rocky bottom
(D) light-shelled snails in a calm inlet with a dark, rocky bottom and many predators
(E) light-shelled snails in a calm inlet with a white, sandy bottom and many predators

8. Measurements of the extent of amino-acid decomposition in fragments of eggshell found at archaeological sites in such places as southern Africa can be used to obtain accurate dates for sites up to 200,000 years old. Because the decomposition is slower in cool climates, the technique can be used to obtain accurate dates for sites almost a million years old in cooler regions.

The information above provides the most support for which one of the following conclusions?

(A) The oldest archaeological sites are not in southern Africa, but rather in cooler regions of the world.
(B) The amino-acid decomposition that enables eggshells to be used in dating does not take place in other organic matter found at ancient archaeological sites.
(C) If the site being dated has been subject to large unsuspected climatic fluctuations during the time the eggshell has been at the site, application of the technique is less likely to yield accurate results.
(D) After 200,000 years in a cool climate, less than one-fifth of the amino acids in a fragment of eggshell that would provide material for dating with the technique will have decomposed and will thus no longer be suitable for examination by the technique.
(E) Fragments of eggshell are more likely to be found at ancient archaeological sites in warm regions of the world than at such sites in cooler regions.

GO ON TO THE NEXT PAGE.

9. Advertisement: Clark brand-name parts are made for cars manufactured in this country. They satisfy all of our government automotive tests—the toughest such tests in the world. With foreign-made parts, you never know which might be reliable and which are cheap look-alikes that are poorly constructed and liable to cost you hundreds of dollars in repairs. Therefore, be smart and insist on brand-name parts by Clark for your car.

    The argument requires the assumption that

    (A)   Clark parts are available only in this country
    (B)   foreign-made parts are not suitable for cars manufactured in this country
    (C)   no foreign-made parts satisfy our government standards
    (D)   parts that satisfy our government standards are not as poorly constructed as cheap foreign-made parts
    (E)   if parts are made for cars manufactured in our country, they are not poorly constructed

10. Even if a crime that has been committed by computer is discovered and reported, the odds of being both arrested and convicted greatly favor the criminal.

    Each of the following, if true, supports the claim above EXCEPT:

    (A)   The preparation of computer-fraud cases takes much more time than is required for average fraud cases, and the productivity of prosecutors is evaluated by the number of good cases made.
    (B)   In most police departments, officers are rotated through different assignments every two or three years, a shorter time than it takes to become proficient as a computer-crime investigator.
    (C)   The priorities of local police departments, under whose jurisdiction most computer crime falls, are weighted toward visible street crime that communities perceive as threatening.
    (D)   Computer criminals have rarely been sentenced to serve time in prison, because prisons are overcrowded with violent criminals and drug offenders.
    (E)   The many police officers who are untrained in computers often inadvertently destroy the physical evidence of computer crime.

11. Every week, the programming office at an FM radio station reviewed unsolicited letters from listeners who were expressing comments on the station's programs. One week, the station received 50 letters with favorable comments about the station's news reporting and music selection and 10 letters with unfavorable comments on the station's new movie review segment of the evening program. Faced with this information, the programming director assumed that if some listeners did not like the movie review segment, then there must be other listeners who did like it. Therefore, he decided to continue the movie review segment of the evening program.

    Which one of the following identifies a problem with the programming director's decision process?

    (A)   He failed to recognize that people are more likely to write letters of criticism than of praise.
    (B)   He could not properly infer from the fact that some listeners did not like the movie review segment that some others did.
    (C)   He failed to take into consideration the discrepancy in numbers between favorable and unfavorable letters received.
    (D)   He failed to take into account the relation existing between the movie review segment and the news.
    (E)   He did not wait until he received at least 50 letters with unfavorable comments about the movie review segment before making his decision.

GO ON TO THE NEXT PAGE.

12. "Though they soon will, patients should not have a legal right to see their medical records. As a doctor, I see two reasons for this. First, giving them access will be time-wasting because it will significantly reduce the amount of time that medical staff can spend on more important duties, by forcing them to retrieve and return files. Second, if my experience is anything to go by, no patients are going to ask for access to their records anyway."

Which one of the following, if true, establishes that the doctor's second reason does not cancel out the first?

(A) The new law will require that doctors, when seeing a patient in their office, must be ready to produce the patient's records immediately, not just ready to retrieve them.
(B) The task of retrieving and returning files would fall to the lowest-paid member of a doctor's office staff.
(C) Any patients who asked to see their medical records would also insist on having details they did not understand explained to them.
(D) The new law does not rule out that doctors may charge patients for extra expenses incurred specifically in order to comply with the new law.
(E) Some doctors have all along had a policy of allowing their patients access to their medical records, but those doctors' patients took no advantage of this policy.

13. Alia: Hawthorne admits that he has influence with high government officials. He further admits that he sold that influence to an environmental interest group. There can be no justification for this kind of unethical behavior.

Martha: I disagree that he was unethical. The group that retained Hawthorne's services is dedicated to the cause of preventing water pollution. So, in using his influence to benefit this group, Hawthorne also benefited the public.

Alia and Martha disagree on whether

(A) the meaning of ethical behavior has changed over time
(B) the consequences of Hawthorne's behavior can ethically justify that behavior
(C) the standards for judging ethical behavior can be imposed on Hawthorne by another
(D) the meaning of ethical behavior is the same in a public situation as in a private one
(E) the definition of ethical behavior is rooted in philosophy or religion

14. The mayor boasts that the average ambulance turnaround time, the time from summons to delivery of the patient, has been reduced this year for top-priority emergencies. This is a serious misrepresentation. This "reduction" was produced simply by redefining "top priority." Such emergencies used to include gunshot wounds and electrocutions, the most time-consuming cases. Now they are limited strictly to heart attacks and strokes.

Which one of the following would strengthen the author's conclusion that it was the redefinition of "top priority" that produced the reduction in turnaround time?

(A) The number of heart attacks and strokes declined this year.
(B) The mayor redefined the city's financial priorities this year.
(C) Experts disagree with the mayor's definition of "top-priority emergency."
(D) Other cities include gunshot wound cases in their category of top-priority emergencies.
(E) One half of all of last year's top-priority emergencies were gunshot wounds and electrocution cases.

15. In a large residential building, there is a rule that no pets are allowed. A group of pet lovers tried to change that rule but failed. The rule-changing procedure outlined in the building's regulations states that only if a group of tenants can obtain the signatures of 10 percent of the tenants on a petition to change a rule will the proposed change be put to a majority vote of all the tenants in the building. It follows that the pet lovers were voted down on their proposal by the majority of the tenants.

The argument depends on which one of the following assumptions?

(A) The pet lovers succeeded in obtaining the signatures of 10 percent of the tenants on their petition.
(B) The signatures of less than 10 percent of the tenants were obtained on the pet lovers' petition.
(C) Ninety percent of the tenants are against changing the rule forbidding pets.
(D) The support of 10 percent of the tenants for a rule change ensures that the rule change will be adopted.
(E) The failure of the pet lovers to obtain the signatures of 10 percent of the tenants on their petition for a rule change ensures that the rule change will be voted down by a majority of the tenants.

GO ON TO THE NEXT PAGE.

16. Nuclear fusion is a process whereby the nuclei of atoms are joined, or "fused," and in which energy is released. One of the by-products of fusion is helium-4 gas. A recent fusion experiment was conducted using "heavy" water contained in a sealed flask. The flask was, in turn, contained in an air-filled chamber designed to eliminate extraneous vibration. After the experiment, a measurable amount of helium-4 gas was found in the air of the chamber. The experimenters cited this evidence in support of their conclusion that fusion had been achieved.

Which one of the following, if true, would cast doubt on the experimenters' conclusion?

(A) Helium-4 was not the only gas found in the experiment chamber.

(B) When fusion is achieved, it normally produces several by-products, including tritium and gamma rays.

(C) The amount of helium-4 found in the chamber's air did not exceed the amount of helium-4 that is found in ordinary air.

(D) Helium-4 gas rapidly breaks down, forming ordinary helium gas after a few hours.

(E) Nuclear fusion reactions are characterized by the release of large amounts of heat.

17. Every photograph, because it involves the light rays that something emits hitting film, must in some obvious sense be true. But because it could always have been made to show things differently than it does, it cannot express the whole truth and, in that sense, is false. Therefore, nothing can ever be definitively proved with a photograph.

Which one of the following is an assumption that would permit the conclusion above to be properly drawn?

(A) Whatever is false in the sense that it cannot express the whole truth cannot furnish definitive proof.

(B) The whole truth cannot be known.

(C) It is not possible to determine the truthfulness of a photograph in any sense.

(D) It is possible to use a photograph as corroborative evidence if there is additional evidence establishing the truth about the scene photographed.

(E) If something is being photographed, then it is possible to prove definitively the truth about it.

GO ON TO THE NEXT PAGE.

Questions 18-19

Some cleaning fluids, synthetic carpets, wall paneling, and other products release toxins, such as formaldehyde and benzene, into the household air supply. This is not a problem in well-ventilated houses, but it is a problem in houses that are so well insulated that they trap toxins as well as heat. Recent tests, however, demonstrate that houseplants remove some household toxins from the air and thereby eliminate their danger. In one test, 20 large plants eliminated formaldehyde from a small, well-insulated house.

18. Assume that a person who lives in a small, well-insulated house that contains toxin-releasing products places houseplants, such as those tested, in the house.

   Which one of the following can be expected as a result?

   (A) There will no longer be any need to ventilate the house.
   (B) The concentration of toxins in the household air supply will remain the same.
   (C) The house will be warm and have a safe air supply.
   (D) If there is formaldehyde in the household air supply, its level will decrease.
   (E) If formaldehyde and benzene are being released into the household air supply, the quantities released of each will decrease.

19. The passage is structured to lead to which one of the following conclusions?

   (A) Houseplants can remove benzene from the air.
   (B) Nonsynthetic products do not release toxins into houses.
   (C) Keeping houseplants is an effective means of trapping heat in a poorly insulated house.
   (D) Keeping houseplants can compensate for some of the negative effects of poor ventilation.
   (E) The air in a well-insulated house with houseplants will contain fewer toxins than the air in a well-ventilated house without houseplants.

20. Normal full-term babies are all born with certain instinctive reflexes that disappear by the age of two months. Because this three-month-old baby exhibits these reflexes, this baby is not a normal full-term baby.

   Which one of the following has a logical structure most like that of the argument above?

   (A) Because carbon dioxide turns limewater milky and this gas is oxygen, it will not turn limewater milky.
   (B) Because no ape can talk and Suzy is an ape, Suzy cannot talk.
   (C) Because humans are social animals and Henry is sociable, Henry is normal.
   (D) Because opossums have abdominal pouches and this animal lacks any such pouch, this animal is not an opossum.
   (E) Because some types of trees shed their leaves annually and this tree has not shed its leaves, it is not normal.

21. Efficiency and redundancy are contradictory characteristics of linguistic systems; however, they can be used together to achieve usefulness and reliability in communication. If a spoken language is completely efficient, then every possible permutation of its basic language sounds can be an understandable word. However, if the human auditory system is an imperfect receptor of sounds, then it is not true that every possible permutation of a spoken language's basic language sounds can be an understandable word.

   If all of the statements above are true, which one of the following must also be true?

   (A) Efficiency causes a spoken language to be useful and redundancy causes it to be reliable.
   (B) Neither efficiency nor redundancy can be completely achieved in spoken language.
   (C) If a spoken language were completely redundant, then it could not be useful.
   (D) If the human auditory system were a perfect receptor of sounds, then every permutation of language sounds would be an understandable word.
   (E) If the human auditory system is an imperfect receptor of sounds, then a spoken language cannot be completely efficient.

GO ON TO THE NEXT PAGE.

22. All intelligent people are nearsighted. I am very nearsighted. So I must be a genius.

    Which one of the following exhibits both of the logical flaws exhibited in the argument above?

    (A) I must be stupid because all intelligent people are nearsighted and I have perfect eyesight.
    (B) All chickens have beaks. This bird has a beak. So this bird must be a chicken.
    (C) All pigs have four legs, but this spider has eight legs. So this spider must be twice as big as any pig.
    (D) John is extremely happy, so he must be extremely tall because all tall people are happy.
    (E) All geniuses are very nearsighted. I must be very nearsighted since I am a genius.

23. An advertisement states:
    Like Danaxil, all headache pills can stop your headache. But when you are in pain, you want relief right away. Danaxil is for you—no headache pill stops pain more quickly.
    Evelyn and Jane are each suffering from a headache. Suppose Evelyn takes Danaxil and Jane takes its leading competitor. Which one of the following can be properly concluded from the claims in the advertisement?

    (A) Evelyn's headache pain will be relieved, but Jane's will not.
    (B) Evelyn's headache pain will be relieved more quickly than Jane's.
    (C) Evelyn's headache will be relieved at least as quickly as Jane's.
    (D) Jane's headache pain will be relieved at the same time as is Evelyn's.
    (E) Jane will be taking Danaxil for relief from headache pain.

Questions 24–25

In opposing the 1970 Clean Air Act, the United States automobile industry argued that meeting the act's standards for automobile emissions was neither economically feasible nor environmentally necessary. However, the catalytic converter, invented in 1967, enabled automakers to meet the 1970 standards efficiently. Currently, automakers are lobbying against the government's attempt to pass legislation that would tighten restrictions on automobile emissions. The automakers contend that these new restrictions would be overly expensive and unnecessary to efforts to curb air pollution. Clearly, the automobile industry's position should not be heeded.

24. Which one of the following most accurately expresses the method used to counter the automakers' current position?

    (A) The automakers' premises are shown to lead to a contradiction.
    (B) Facts are mentioned that show that the automakers are relying on false information.
    (C) A flaw is pointed out in the reasoning used by the automakers to reach their conclusion.
    (D) A comparison is drawn between the automakers' current position and a position they held in the past.
    (E) Evidence is provided that the new emissions legislation is both economically feasible and environmentally necessary.

25. Which one of the following, if true, lends the most support to the automakers' current position?

    (A) The more stringent the legislation restricting emissions becomes, the more difficult it becomes for automakers to provide the required technology economically.
    (B) Emissions-restriction technology can often be engineered so as to avoid reducing the efficiency with which an automobile uses fuel.
    (C) Not every new piece of legislation restricting emissions requires new automotive technology in order for automakers to comply with it.
    (D) The more automobiles there are on the road, the more stringent emission restrictions must be to prevent increased overall air pollution.
    (E) Unless forced to do so by the government, automakers rarely make changes in automotive technology that is not related to profitability.

S T O P

IF YOU FINISH BEFORE TIME IS CALLED, YOU MAY CHECK YOUR WORK ON THIS SECTION ONLY.
DO NOT WORK ON ANY OTHER SECTION IN THE TEST.

Acknowledgment is made to the following for permission to reprint selections that appear in PrepTest II:

From "Striking the Balance: Congress and the President Under the War Powers Resolution" by Cyrus R. Vance. *University of Pennsylvania Law Review*, Volume 133, Number 1, December 1984. © 1984 by the University of Pennsylvania. Used by permission.

SIGNATURE ————————————————————————————

DATE

LSAT WRITING SAMPLE TOPIC

The large publishing firm that owns financially troubled Westerly Books has allocated $50,000 to the small company in one major effort to save it. Write an argument for spending the money on one of the following plans. The publishing firm has set the following conditions for keeping Westerly in business:

- Westerly must show a profit within one year by significantly increasing total sales.
- Westerly must change its image from an elite literary press to one with a broader audience appeal.

The Series Plan calls for contracting with a commercial artist who designs covers and book jackets. Westerly primarily publishes fiction by young and little-known writers whose names are recognized by only a small reading audience. This artist successfully launched a series of biographies for another small press by designing distinctive covers that became a trademark for the series. She believes that she can do something similar for Westerly by developing individual cover designs that will also become recognized trademarks. Book stores have told Westerly that its covers lack visual appeal and estimate that sales of its twenty current titles could jump at least 50 percent with better designs. The artist wants a $50,000 contract to undertake this project.

The Star Plan calls for spending the money on promotion of one promising novel. Westerly's books are generally well received by the critics but rarely sell more than five thousand copies. Westerly usually does not have the resources for extensive national advertising. As a result, young writers who start out with Westerly usually sign with larger publishing houses once they achieve some success. Westerly has published two novels by a writer whose popularity has grown steadily. He is about to complete his third novel and claims that, with the right promotion, sales of this novel alone will exceed those of Westerly's entire line. Though optimistic, Westerly's staff has a more conservative estimate of expected sales. To remain with Westerly, the author wants a promotional campaign costing the entire $50,000.

Directions:

1. Use the Answer Key on the next page to check your answers.

2. Use the Scoring Worksheet below to compute your raw score.

3. Use the Score Conversion Chart to convert your raw score into the 120-180 scale.

Scoring Worksheet

1. Enter the number of questions you answered correctly in each section.

	Number Correct
SECTION I	24
SECTION II	_____
SECTION III	_____
SECTION IV	_____

2. Enter the sum here: _____
   This is your Raw Score.

Conversion Chart
Form 2LSS12

For Converting Raw Score to the 120-180 LSAT Scaled Score

Reported Score	Raw Score Lowest	Raw Score Highest
180	100	101
179	99	99
178	98	98
177	97	97
176	—*	—*
175	96	96
174	95	95
173	94	94
172	93	93
171	92	92
170	91	91
169	89	90
168	88	88
167	87	87
166	85	86
165	84	84
164	82	83
163	81	81
162	79	80
161	77	78
160	75	76
159	74	74
158	72	73
157	70	71
156	68	69
155	66	67
154	65	65
153	63	64
152	61	62
151	59	60
150	57	58
149	55	56
148	54	54
147	52	53
146	50	51
145	48	49
144	47	47
143	45	46
142	43	44
141	42	42
140	40	41
139	38	39
138	37	37
137	35	36
136	34	34
135	33	33
134	31	32
133	30	30
132	29	29
131	28	28
130	27	27
129	25	26
128	24	24
127	23	23
126	—*	—*
125	22	22
124	21	21
123	20	20
122	19	19
121	18	18
120	0	17

*There is no raw score that will produce this scaled score for this form.

SECTION I

1.	C	8.	B	15.	D	22.	B
2.	B	9.	B	16.	A	23.	E
3.	D	10.	E	17.	A	24.	B
4.	B	11.	C	18.	B	25.	B
5.	A	12.	D	19.	E	26.	C
6.	D	13.	A	20.	C	27.	A
7.	E	14.	D	21.	A	28.	D

SECTION II

1.	D	8.	E	15.	B	22.	A
2.	E	9.	B	16.	E	23.	E
3.	E	10.	C	17.	B	24.	E
4.	D	11.	B	18.	B		
5.	C	12.	A	19.	D		
6.	B	13.	C	20.	C		
7.	A	14.	C	21.	D		

SECTION III

1.	D	8.	A	15.	D	22.	E
2.	A	9.	E	16.	B	23.	B
3.	A	10.	C	17.	C	24.	D
4.	E	11.	B	18.	E		
5.	D	12.	C	19.	B		
6.	D	13.	A	20.	E		
7.	E	14.	D	21.	A		

SECTION IV

1.	C	8.	C	15.	A	22.	D
2.	C	9.	D	16.	C	23.	C
3.	E	10.	D	17.	A	24.	D
4.	A	11.	B	18.	D	25.	A
5.	B	12.	A	19.	D		
6.	B	13.	B	20.	D		
7.	D	14.	E	21.	E		

The Official

LSAT

PrepTest™ IV

The sample test that follows consists of
four sections corresponding to the four
scored sections of the February 1992 LSAT.

February 1992
Form 2LSS15

General Directions for the LSAT Answer Sheet

The actual testing time for this portion of the test will be 2 hours 55 minutes. There are five sections, each with a time limit of 35 minutes. The supervisor will tell you when to begin and end each section. If you finish a section before time is called, you may check your work on that section <u>only</u>; do not turn to any other section of the test book and do not work on any other section either in the test book or on the answer sheet.

There are several different types of questions on the test, and each question type has its own directions. <u>Be sure you understand the directions for each question type before attempting to answer any questions in that section.</u>

Not everyone will finish all the questions in the time allowed. Do not hurry, but work steadily and as quickly as you can without sacrificing accuracy. You are advised to use your time effectively. If a question seems too difficult, go on to the next one and return to the difficult question after completing the section. MARK THE BEST ANSWER YOU CAN FOR EVERY QUESTION. NO DEDUCTIONS WILL BE MADE FOR WRONG ANSWERS. YOUR SCORE WILL BE BASED ONLY ON THE NUMBER OF QUESTIONS YOU ANSWER CORRECTLY.

ALL YOUR ANSWERS MUST BE MARKED ON THE ANSWER SHEET. Answer spaces for each question are lettered to correspond with the letters of the potential answers to each question in the test book. After you have decided which of the answers is correct, blacken the corresponding space on the answer sheet. BE SURE THAT EACH MARK IS BLACK AND COMPLETELY FILLS THE ANSWER SPACE. Give only one answer to each question. If you change an answer, be sure that all previous marks are <u>erased completely</u>. Since the answer sheet is machine scored, incomplete erasures may be interpreted as intended answers. ANSWERS RECORDED IN THE TEST BOOK WILL NOT BE SCORED.

There may be more questions noted on this answer sheet than there are questions in a section. Do not be concerned but be certain that the section and number of the question you are answering matches the answer sheet section and question number. Additional answer spaces in any answer sheet section should be left blank. Begin your next section in the number one answer space for that section.

Score Cancellation

Complete this section only if you are absolutely certain you want to cancel your score. A CANCELLATION REQUEST CANNOT BE RESCINDED. IF YOU ARE AT ALL UNCERTAIN, YOU SHOULD NOT COMPLETE THIS SECTION; INSTEAD, YOU SHOULD USE THE TIME ALLOWED AFTER THE TEST (UP TO 5 DAYS) TO FULLY CONSIDER YOUR DECISION.

To cancel your score from this administration, you must:

A. fill in the ovals here........ ◯ ◯

B. read the following statement. Then sign your name and enter the date.

I certify that I wish to cancel my test score from this administration. I understand that my request is irreversible and that my score will not be sent to me or to the law schools to which I apply.

_____
Sign your name in full

_____
Date

HOW DID YOU PREPARE FOR THE LSAT?
(Select all that apply.)

Responses to this item are voluntary and will be used for statistical research purposes only.

- ◯ By studying the sample questions in the *LSAT/LSDAS Registration and Information Book*.
- ◯ By taking the free sample LSAT.
- ◯ By working through *The Official LSAT PrepTest(s), PrepBook, Workbooks, or PrepKit*.
- ◯ By using a book on how to prepare for the LSAT **not** published by Law Services.
- ◯ By attending a commercial test preparation or coaching course.
- ◯ By attending a test preparation or coaching course offered through an undergraduate institution.
- ◯ Self study.
- ◯ Other preparation.
- ◯ No preparation.

CERTIFYING STATEMENT

Please write (DO NOT PRINT) the following statement. Sign and date.

I certify that I am the examinee whose name appears on this answer sheet and that I am here to take the LSAT for the sole purpose of being considered for admission to law school. I further certify that I will neither assist nor receive assistance from any other candidate, and I agree not to copy or retain examination questions or to transmit them in any form to any other person.

_____
_____
_____
_____
_____
_____
_____
_____
_____

SIGNATURE: _____ TODAY'S DATE: ___ / ___ / ___
                                                         MONTH DAY YEAR

INSTRUCTIONS FOR COMPLETING THE BIOGRAPHICAL AREA ARE ON THE BACK COVER OF YOUR TEST BOOKLET.
USE ONLY A NO. 2 OR HB PENCIL TO COMPLETE THIS ANSWER SHEET. DO NOT USE INK.

1 LAST NAME · FIRST NAME · MI

(A through Z bubbles for each letter position)

2 DATE OF BIRTH

MONTH	DAY	YEAR
Jan		
Feb		
Mar	0 0	0 0
Apr	1 1	1 1
May	2 2	2 2
June	3 3	3 3
July	4	4 4
Aug	5 5	5 5
Sept	6 6	6 6
Oct	7 7	7 7
Nov	8 8	8 8
Dec	9 9	9 9

3 SOCIAL SECURITY NO.

(0–9 bubbles)

Right Mark: ●
Wrong Marks: ⊘ ⊗ ⊙

4 ETHNIC DESCRIPTION

- American Indian/ Alaskan Native
- Asian/Pacific Islander
- Black/African Amer.
- Canadian Aboriginal
- Caucasian/White
- Chicano/Mex. Amer.
- Hispanic
- Puerto Rican
- Other

5 GENDER
- Male
- Female

6 DOMINANT LANGUAGE
- English
- Other

7 ENGLISH FLUENCY
- Yes
- No

8 CENTER NUMBER

(0–9 bubbles)

9 TEST FORM CODE

(0–9 bubbles)

10 TEST BOOK SERIAL NO.

11 TEST FORM

12 TEST DATE

MONTH / DAY / YEAR

13 PLEASE PRINT ALL INFORMATION

LAST NAME   FIRST

MAILING ADDRESS

SOCIAL SECURITY/ SOCIAL INSURANCE NO.

NOTE: If you have a new address, you must write Law Services at Box 2000-C, Newtown, PA 18940 or call (215) 968-1001. We cannot guarantee that all address changes will be processed before scores are mailed, so be sure to notify your post office of your forwarding address.

LAW SCHOOL ADMISSION TEST

MARK ONE AND ONLY ONE ANSWER TO EACH QUESTION. BE SURE TO FILL IN COMPLETELY THE SPACE FOR YOUR INTENDED ANSWER CHOICE. IF YOU ERASE, DO SO COMPLETELY. MAKE NO STRAY MARKS.

SECTION 1	SECTION 2	SECTION 3	SECTION 4	SECTION 5
1 A B C D E	1 A B C D E	1 A B C D E	1 A B C D E	1 A B C D E
2 A B C D E	2 A B C D E	2 A B C D E	2 A B C D E	2 A B C D E
3 A B C D E	3 A B C D E	3 A B C D E	3 A B C D E	3 A B C D E
4 A B C D E	4 A B C D E	4 A B C D E	4 A B C D E	4 A B C D E
5 A B C D E	5 A B C D E	5 A B C D E	5 A B C D E	5 A B C D E
6 A B C D E	6 A B C D E	6 A B C D E	6 A B C D E	6 A B C D E
7 A B C D E	7 A B C D E	7 A B C D E	7 A B C D E	7 A B C D E
8 A B C D E	8 A B C D E	8 A B C D E	8 A B C D E	8 A B C D E
9 A B C D E	9 A B C D E	9 A B C D E	9 A B C D E	9 A B C D E
10 A B C D E	10 A B C D E	10 A B C D E	10 A B C D E	10 A B C D E
11 A B C D E	11 A B C D E	11 A B C D E	11 A B C D E	11 A B C D E
12 A B C D E	12 A B C D E	12 A B C D E	12 A B C D E	12 A B C D E
13 A B C D E	13 A B C D E	13 A B C D E	13 A B C D E	13 A B C D E
14 A B C D E	14 A B C D E	14 A B C D E	14 A B C D E	14 A B C D E
15 A B C D E	15 A B C D E	15 A B C D E	15 A B C D E	15 A B C D E
16 A B C D E	16 A B C D E	16 A B C D E	16 A B C D E	16 A B C D E
17 A B C D E	17 A B C D E	17 A B C D E	17 A B C D E	17 A B C D E
18 A B C D E	18 A B C D E	18 A B C D E	18 A B C D E	18 A B C D E
19 A B C D E	19 A B C D E	19 A B C D E	19 A B C D E	19 A B C D E
20 A B C D E	20 A B C D E	20 A B C D E	20 A B C D E	20 A B C D E
21 A B C D E	21 A B C D E	21 A B C D E	21 A B C D E	21 A B C D E
22 A B C D E	22 A B C D E	22 A B C D E	22 A B C D E	22 A B C D E
23 A B C D E	23 A B C D E	23 A B C D E	23 A B C D E	23 A B C D E
24 A B C D E	24 A B C D E	24 A B C D E	24 A B C D E	24 A B C D E
25 A B C D E	25 A B C D E	25 A B C D E	25 A B C D E	25 A B C D E
26 A B C D E	26 A B C D E	26 A B C D E	26 A B C D E	26 A B C D E
27 A B C D E	27 A B C D E	27 A B C D E	27 A B C D E	27 A B C D E
28 A B C D E	28 A B C D E	28 A B C D E	28 A B C D E	28 A B C D E
29 A B C D E	29 A B C D E	29 A B C D E	29 A B C D E	29 A B C D E
30 A B C D E	30 A B C D E	30 A B C D E	30 A B C D E	30 A B C D E

FOR LAW SERVICES USE ONLY
LR
LW
LCS

SECTION I

Time—35 minutes

24 Questions

Directions: The questions in this section are based on the reasoning contained in brief statements or passages. For some questions, more than one of the choices could conceivably answer the question. However, you are to choose the best answer; that is, the response that most accurately and completely answers the question. You should not make assumptions that are by commonsense standards implausible, superfluous, or incompatible with the passage. After you have chosen the best answer, blacken the corresponding space on your answer sheet.

1. Rita: The original purpose of government farm-subsidy programs was to provide income stability for small family farmers, but most farm-subsidy money goes to a few farmers with large holdings. Payments to farmers whose income, before subsidies, is greater than $100,000 a year should be stopped.

   Thomas: It would be impossible to administer such a cutoff point. Subsidies are needed during the planting and growing season, but farmers do not know their income for a given calendar year until tax returns are calculated and submitted the following April.

   Which one of the following, if true, is the strongest counter Rita can make to Thomas' objection?

   (A) It has become difficult for small farmers to obtain bank loans to be repaid later by money from subsidies.
   (B) Having such a cutoff point would cause some farmers whose income would otherwise exceed $100,000 to reduce their plantings.
   (C) The income of a farmer varies because weather and market prices are not stable from year to year.
   (D) If subsidy payments to large farmers were eliminated, the financial condition of the government would improve.
   (E) Subsidy cutoffs can be determined on the basis of income for the preceding year.

2. Modern physicians often employ laboratory tests, in addition to physical examinations, in order to diagnose diseases accurately. Insurance company regulations that deny coverage for certain laboratory tests therefore decrease the quality of medical care provided to patients.

   Which one of the following is an assumption that would serve to justify the conclusion above?

   (A) Physical examinations and the uncovered laboratory tests together provide a more accurate diagnosis of many diseases than do physical examinations alone.
   (B) Many physicians generally oppose insurance company regulations that, in order to reduce costs, limit the use of laboratory tests.
   (C) Many patients who might benefit from the uncovered laboratory tests do not have any form of health insurance.
   (D) There are some illnesses that experienced physicians can diagnose accurately from physical examination alone.
   (E) Laboratory tests are more costly to perform than are physical examinations.

3. Oil analysts predict that if the price of oil falls by half, the consumer's purchase price for gasoline made from this oil will also fall by half.

   Which one of the following, if true, would cast the most serious doubt on the prediction made by the oil analysts?

   (A) Improved automobile technology and new kinds of fuel for cars have enabled some drivers to use less gasoline.
   (B) Gasoline manufacturers will not expand their profit margins.
   (C) There are many different gasoline companies that compete with each other to provide the most attractive price to consumers.
   (D) Studies in several countries show that the amount of gasoline purchased by consumers initially rises after the price of gasoline has fallen.
   (E) Refining costs, distribution costs, and taxes, none of which varies significantly with oil prices, constitute a large portion of the price of gasoline.

GO ON TO THE NEXT PAGE.

4. A survey was recently conducted among ferry passengers on the North Sea. Among the results was this: more of those who had taken anti-seasickness medication before their trip reported symptoms of seasickness than those who had not taken such medication. It is clear, then, that despite claims by drug companies that clinical tests show the contrary, people would be better off not taking anti-seasickness medications.

Which one of the following, if true, would most weaken the conclusion above?

(A) Given rough enough weather, most ferry passengers will have some symptoms of seasickness.
(B) The clinical tests reported by the drug companies were conducted by the drug companies' staffs.
(C) People who do not take anti-seasickness medication are just as likely to respond to a survey on seasickness as people who do.
(D) The seasickness symptoms of the people who took anti-seasickness medication would have been more severe had they not taken the medication.
(E) People who have spent money on anti-seasickness medication are less likely to admit symptoms of seasickness than those who have not.

5. Economic considerations color every aspect of international dealings, and nations are just like individuals in that the lender sets the terms of its dealings with the borrower. That is why a nation that owes money to another nation cannot be a world leader.

The reasoning in the passage assumes which one of the following?

(A) A nation that does not lend to any other nation cannot be a world leader.
(B) A nation that can set the terms of its dealings with other nations is certain to be a world leader.
(C) A nation that has the terms of its dealings with another nation set by that nation cannot be a world leader.
(D) A nation that is a world leader can borrow from another nation as long as that other nation does not set the terms of the dealings between the two nations.
(E) A nation that has no dealings with any other nation cannot be a world leader.

Questions 6–7

Rotelle: You are too old to address effectively the difficult issues facing the country, such as nuclear power, poverty, and pollution.
Sims: I don't want to make age an issue in this campaign, so I will not comment on your youth and inexperience.

6. Sims does which one of the following?

(A) demonstrates that Rotelle's claim is incorrect
(B) avoids mentioning the issue of age
(C) proposes a way to decide which issues are important
(D) shows that Rotelle's statement is self-contradictory
(E) fails to respond directly to Rotelle's claim

7. Rotelle is committed to which one of the following?

(A) Many old people cannot effectively address the difficult issues facing the country.
(B) Those at least as old as Sims are the only people who cannot effectively address the difficult issues facing the country.
(C) Some young people can effectively address the difficult issues facing the country.
(D) If anyone can effectively address the difficult issues facing the country, that person must be younger than Sims.
(E) Addressing the difficult issues facing the country requires an understanding of young people's points of view.

GO ON TO THE NEXT PAGE.

8. Political theorist: The chief foundations of all governments are the legal system and the police force; and as there cannot be a good legal system where the police are not well paid, it follows that where the police are well paid there will be a good legal system.

The reasoning in the argument is not sound because it fails to establish that

(A) many governments with bad legal systems have poorly paid police forces
(B) bad governments with good legal systems must have poorly paid police forces
(C) a well-paid police force cannot be effective without a good legal system
(D) a well-paid police force is sufficient to guarantee a good legal system
(E) some bad governments have good legal systems

9. Court records from medieval France show that in the years 1300 to 1400 the number of people arrested in the French realm for "violent interpersonal crimes" (not committed in wars) increased by 30 percent over the number of people arrested for such crimes in the years 1200 to 1300. If the increase was not the result of false arrests, therefore, medieval France had a higher level of documented interpersonal violence in the years 1300 to 1400 than in the years 1200 to 1300.

Which one of the following statements, if true, most seriously weakens the argument?

(A) In the years 1300 to 1400 the French government's category of violent crimes included an increasing variety of interpersonal crimes that are actually nonviolent.
(B) Historical accounts by monastic chroniclers in the years 1300 to 1400 are filled with descriptions of violent attacks committed by people living in the French realm.
(C) The number of individual agreements between two people in which they swore oaths not to attack each other increased substantially after 1300.
(D) When English armies tried to conquer parts of France in the mid- to late 1300s, violence in the northern province of Normandy and the southwestern province of Gascony increased.
(E) The population of medieval France increased substantially during the first five decades of the 1300s, until the deadly bubonic plague decimated the population of France after 1348.

10. *Rhizobium* bacteria living in the roots of bean plants or other legumes produce fixed nitrogen, which is one of the essential plant nutrients and which for non-legume crops, such as wheat, normally must be supplied by applications of nitrogen-based fertilizer. So if biotechnology succeeds in producing wheat strains whose roots will play host to *Rhizobium* bacteria, the need for artificial fertilizers will be reduced.

The argument above makes which one of the following assumptions?

(A) Biotechnology should be directed toward producing plants that do not require artificial fertilizer.
(B) Fixed nitrogen is currently the only soil nutrient that must be supplied by artificial fertilizer for growing wheat crops.
(C) There are no naturally occurring strains of wheat or other grasses that have *Rhizobium* bacteria living in their roots.
(D) Legumes are currently the only crops that produce their own supply of fixed nitrogen.
(E) *Rhizobium* bacteria living in the roots of wheat would produce fixed nitrogen.

11. Current legislation that requires designated sections for smokers and nonsmokers on the premises of privately owned businesses is an intrusion into the private sector that cannot be justified. The fact that studies indicate that nonsmokers might be harmed by inhaling the smoke from others' cigarettes is not the main issue. Rather, the main issue concerns the government's violation of the right of private businesses to determine their own policies and rules.

Which one of the following is a principle that, if accepted, could enable the conclusion to be properly drawn?

(A) Government intrusion into the policies and rules of private businesses is justified only when individuals might be harmed.
(B) The right of individuals to breathe safe air supersedes the right of businesses to be free from government intrusion.
(C) The right of businesses to self-determination overrides whatever right or duty the government may have to protect the individual.
(D) It is the duty of private businesses to protect employees from harm in the workplace.
(E) Where the rights of businesses and the duty of government conflict, the main issue is finding a successful compromise.

GO ON TO THE NEXT PAGE.

12. Leachate is a solution, frequently highly contaminated, that develops when water permeates a landfill site. If and only if the landfill's capacity to hold liquids is exceeded does the leachate escape into the environment, generally in unpredictable quantities. A method must be found for disposing of leachate. Most landfill leachate is sent directly to sewage treatment plants, but not all sewage plants are capable of handling the highly contaminated water.

Which one of the following can be inferred from the passage?

(A) The ability to predict the volume of escaping landfill leachate would help solve the disposal problem.

(B) If any water permeates a landfill, leachate will escape into the environment.

(C) No sewage treatment plants are capable of handling leachate.

(D) Some landfill leachate is sent to sewage treatment plants that are incapable of handling it.

(E) If leachate does not escape from a landfill into the environment, then the landfill's capacity to hold liquids has not been exceeded.

13. The soaring prices of scholarly and scientific journals have forced academic libraries used only by academic researchers to drastically reduce their list of subscriptions. Some have suggested that in each academic discipline subscription decisions should be determined solely by a journal's usefulness in that discipline, measured by the frequency with which it is cited in published writings by researchers in the discipline.

Which one of the following, if true, most seriously calls into question the suggestion described above?

(A) The nonacademic readership of a scholarly or scientific journal can be accurately gauged by the number of times articles appearing in it are cited in daily newspapers and popular magazines.

(B) The average length of a journal article in some sciences, such as physics, is less than half the average length of a journal article in some other academic disciplines, such as history.

(C) The increasingly expensive scholarly journals are less and less likely to be available to the general public from nonacademic public libraries.

(D) Researchers often will not cite a journal article that has influenced their work if they think that the journal in which it appears is not highly regarded by the leading researchers in the mainstream of the discipline.

(E) In some academic disciplines, controversies which begin in the pages of one journal spill over into articles in other journals that are widely read by researchers in the discipline.

14. The average level of fat in the blood of people suffering from acute cases of disease W is lower than the average level for the population as a whole. Nevertheless, most doctors believe that reducing blood-fat levels is an effective way of preventing acute W.

Which one of the following, if true, does most to justify this apparently paradoxical belief?

(A) The blood level of fat for patients who have been cured of W is on average the same as that for the population at large.

(B) Several of the symptoms characteristic of acute W have been produced in laboratory animals fed large doses of a synthetic fat substitute, though acute W itself has not been produced in this way.

(C) The progression from latent to acute W can occur only when the agent that causes acute W absorbs large quantities of fat from the patient's blood.

(D) The levels of fat in the blood of patients who have disease W respond abnormally slowly to changes in dietary intake of fat.

(E) High levels of fat in the blood are indicative of several diseases that are just as serious as W.

15. Baking for winter holidays is a tradition that may have a sound medical basis. In midwinter, when days are short, many people suffer from a specific type of seasonal depression caused by lack of sunlight. Carbohydrates, both sugars and starches, boost the brain's levels of serotonin, a neurotransmitter that improves the mood. In this respect, carbohydrates act on the brain in the same way as some antidepressants. Thus, eating holiday cookies may provide an effective form of self-prescribed medication.

Which one of the following can be properly inferred from the passage?

(A) Seasonal depression is one of the most easily treated forms of depression.

(B) Lack of sunlight lowers the level of serotonin in the brain.

(C) People are more likely to be depressed in midwinter than at other times of the year.

(D) Some antidepressants act by changing the brain's level of serotonin.

(E) Raising the level of neurotransmitters in the brain effectively relieves depression.

GO ON TO THE NEXT PAGE.

16. The current proposal to give college students a broader choice in planning their own courses of study should be abandoned. The students who are supporting the proposal will never be satisfied, no matter what requirements are established. Some of these students have reached their third year without declaring a major. One first-year student has failed to complete four required courses. Several others have indicated a serious indifference to grades and intellectual achievement.

A flaw in the argument is that it does which one of the following?

(A) avoids the issue by focusing on supporters of the proposal
(B) argues circularly by assuming the conclusion is true in stating the premises
(C) fails to define the critical term "satisfied"
(D) distorts the proposal advocated by opponents
(E) uses the term "student" equivocally

Questions 17–18

The question whether intelligent life exists elsewhere in the universe is certainly imprecise, because we are not sure how different from us something might be and still count as "intelligent life." Yet we cannot just decide to define "intelligent life" in some more precise way since it is likely that we will find and recognize intelligent life elsewhere in the universe only if we leave our definitions open to new, unimagined possibilities.

17. The argument can most reasonably be interpreted as an objection to which one of the following claims?

(A) The question whether intelligent life exists elsewhere in the universe is one that will never be correctly answered.
(B) Whether or not there is intelligent life elsewhere in the universe, our understanding of intelligent life is limited.
(C) The question about the existence of intelligent life elsewhere in the universe must be made more precise if we hope to answer it correctly.
(D) The question whether there is intelligent life elsewhere in the universe is so imprecise as to be meaningless.
(E) The question whether there is intelligent life elsewhere in the universe is one we should not spend our time trying to answer.

18. The passage, if seen as an objection to an antecedent claim, challenges that claim by

(A) showing the claim to be irrelevant to the issue at hand
(B) citing examples that fail to fit a proposed definition of "intelligent life"
(C) claiming that "intelligent life" cannot be adequately defined
(D) arguing that the claim, if acted on, would be counterproductive
(E) maintaining that the claim is not supported by the available evidence

GO ON TO THE NEXT PAGE.

19. The efficiency of microwave ovens in destroying the harmful bacteria frequently found in common foods is diminished by the presence of salt in the food being cooked. When heated in a microwave oven, the interior of unsalted food reaches temperatures high enough to kill bacteria that cause food poisoning, but the interior of salted food does not. Scientists theorize that salt effectively blocks the microwaves from heating the interior.

Which one of the following conclusions is most supported by the information above?

(A) The kinds of bacteria that cause food poisoning are more likely to be found on the exterior of food than in the interior of food.
(B) The incidence of serious food poisoning would be significantly reduced if microwave ovens were not used by consumers to cook or reheat food.
(C) The addition of salt to food that has been cooked or reheated in a microwave oven can increase the danger of food poisoning.
(D) The danger of food poisoning can be lessened if salt is not used to prepare foods that are to be cooked in a microwave oven.
(E) Salt is the primary cause of food poisoning resulting from food that is heated in microwave ovens.

20. Pamela: Business has an interest in enabling employees to care for children, because those children will be the customers, employees, and managers of the future. Therefore, businesses should adopt policies, such as day-care benefits, that facilitate parenting.

Lee: No individual company, though, will be patronized, staffed, and managed only by its own employees' children, so it would not be to a company's advantage to provide such benefits to employees when other companies do not.

In which one of the following pairs consisting of argument and objection does the objection function most similarly to the way Lee's objection functions in relation to Pamela's argument?

(A) New roads will not serve to relieve this area's traffic congestion, because new roads would encourage new construction and generate additional traffic.
    Objection: Failure to build new roads would mean that traffic congestion would strangle the area even earlier.
(B) Humanity needs clean air to breathe, so each person should make an effort to avoid polluting the air.
    Objection: The air one person breathes is affected mainly by pollution caused by others, so it makes no sense to act alone to curb air pollution.
(C) Advertised discounts on products draw customers' attention to the products, so advertised discounts benefit sales.
    Objection: Customers already planning to purchase a product accelerate buying to take advantage of advertised discounts, and thus subsequent sales suffer.
(D) If people always told lies, then no one would know what the truth was, so people should always tell the truth.
    Objection: If people always told lies, then everyone would know that the truth was the opposite of what was said.
(E) Human social institutions have always changed, so even if we do not know what those changes will be, we do know that the social institutions of the future will differ from those of the past.
    Objection: The existence of change in the past does not ensure that there will always be change in the future.

GO ON TO THE NEXT PAGE.

21. Pedro: Unlike cloth diapers, disposable diapers are a threat to the environment. Sixteen billion disposable diapers are discarded annually, filling up landfills at an alarming rate. So people must stop buying disposable diapers and use cloth diapers.

Maria: But you forget that cloth diapers must be washed in hot water, which requires energy. Moreover, the resulting wastewater pollutes our rivers. When families use diaper services, diapers must be delivered by fuel-burning trucks that pollute the air and add to traffic congestion.

Maria objects to Pedro's argument by

(A) claiming that Pedro overstates the negative evidence about disposable diapers in the course of his argument in favor of cloth diapers

(B) indicating that Pedro draws a hasty conclusion, based on inadequate evidence about cloth diapers

(C) pointing out that there is an ambiguous use of the word "disposable" in Pedro's argument

(D) demonstrating that cloth diapers are a far more serious threat to the environment than disposable diapers are

(E) suggesting that the economic advantages of cloth diapers outweigh whatever environmental damage they may cause

22. In an experiment, two-year-old boys and their fathers made pie dough together using rolling pins and other utensils. Each father-son pair used a rolling pin that was distinctively different from those used by the other father-son pairs, and each father repeated the phrase "rolling pin" each time his son used it. But when the children were asked to identify all of the rolling pins among a group of kitchen utensils that included several rolling pins, each child picked only the one that he had used.

Which one of the following inferences is most supported by the information above?

(A) The children did not grasp the function of a rolling pin.

(B) No two children understood the name "rolling pin" to apply to the same object.

(C) The children understood that all rolling pins have the same general shape.

(D) Each child was able to identify correctly only the utensils that he had used.

(E) The children were not able to distinguish the rolling pins they used from other rolling pins.

GO ON TO THE NEXT PAGE.

23. When 100 people who have not used cocaine are tested for cocaine use, on average only 5 will test positive. By contrast, of every 100 people who have used cocaine 99 will test positive. Thus, when a randomly chosen group of people is tested for cocaine use, the vast majority of those who test positive will be people who have used cocaine.

A reasoning error in the argument is that the argument

(A) attempts to infer a value judgment from purely factual premises
(B) attributes to every member of the population the properties of the average member of the population
(C) fails to take into account what proportion of the population have used cocaine
(D) ignores the fact that some cocaine users do not test positive
(E) advocates testing people for cocaine use when there is no reason to suspect that they have used cocaine

24. If a society encourages freedom of thought and expression, then, during the time when it does so, creativity will flourish in that society. In the United States creativity flourished during the eighteenth century. It is clear, therefore, that freedom of thought was encouraged in the United States during the eighteenth century.

An error of reasoning of the same kind as one contained in the passage is present in each of the following arguments EXCEPT:

(A) According to the airline industry, airfares have to rise if air travel is to be made safer; since airfares were just raised, we can rest assured that air travel will therefore become safer.
(B) We can conclude that the Hillside police department has improved its efficiency, because crime rates are down in Hillside, and it is an established fact that crime rates go down when police departments increase their efficiency.
(C) People who are really interested in the preservation of wildlife obviously do not go hunting for big game; since Gerda has never gone hunting for big game and intends never to do so, it is clear that she is really interested in the preservation of wildlife.
(D) If the contents of a bottle are safe to drink, the bottle will not be marked "poison," so, since the bottle is not marked "poison," its contents will be safe to drink.
(E) None of the so-called Western democracies is really democratic, because, for a country to be democratic, the opinion of each of its citizens must have a meaningful effect on government, and in none of these countries does each citizen's opinion have such an effect.

S T O P

IF YOU FINISH BEFORE TIME IS CALLED, YOU MAY CHECK YOUR WORK ON THIS SECTION ONLY.
DO NOT WORK ON ANY OTHER SECTION IN THE TEST.

SECTION II
Time—35 minutes
27 Questions

Directions: Each passage in this section is followed by a group of questions to be answered on the basis of what is stated or implied in the passage. For some of the questions, more than one of the choices could conceivably answer the question. However, you are to choose the best answer; that is, the response that most accurately and completely answers the question, and blacken the corresponding space on your answer sheet.

The extent of a nation's power over its coastal ecosystems and the natural resources in its coastal waters has been defined by two international law doctrines: freedom of the seas and adjacent state
(5) sovereignty. Until the mid-twentieth century, most nations favored application of broad open-seas freedoms and limited sovereign rights over coastal waters. A nation had the right to include within its territorial dominion only a very narrow band of
(10) coastal waters (generally extending three miles from the shoreline), within which it had the authority, but not the responsibility, to regulate all activities. But, because this area of territorial dominion was so limited, most nations did not establish rules for
(15) management or protection of their territorial waters.

Regardless of whether or not nations enforced regulations in their territorial waters, large ocean areas remained free of controls or restrictions. The citizens of all nations had the right to use these
(20) unrestricted ocean areas for any innocent purpose, including navigation and fishing. Except for controls over its own citizens, no nation had the responsibility, let alone the unilateral authority, to control such activities in international waters. And, since there
(25) were few standards of conduct that applied on the "open seas," there were few jurisdictional conflicts between nations.

The lack of standards is traceable to popular perceptions held before the middle of this century.
(30) By and large, marine pollution was not perceived as a significant problem, in part because the adverse effect of coastal activities on ocean ecosystems was not widely recognized, and pollution caused by human activities was generally believed to be limited
(35) to that caused by navigation. Moreover, the freedom to fish, or overfish, was an essential element of the traditional legal doctrine of freedom of the seas that no maritime country wished to see limited. And finally, the technology that later allowed exploitation
(40) of other ocean resources, such as oil, did not yet exist.

To date, controlling pollution and regulating ocean resources have still not been comprehensively addressed by law, but international law—established through the customs and practices of nations—does
(45) not preclude such efforts. And two recent developments may actually lead to future international rules providing for ecosystem management. First, the establishment of extensive fishery zones, extending territorial authority as far as
(50) 200 miles out from a country's coast, has provided the opportunity for nations individually to manage larger ecosystems. This opportunity, combined with national self-interest in maintaining fish populations, could lead nations to reevaluate policies for
(55) management of their fisheries and to address the problem of pollution in territorial waters. Second, the international community is beginning to understand the importance of preserving the resources and ecology of international waters and to show signs of
(60) accepting responsibility for doing so. As an international consensus regarding the need for comprehensive management of ocean resources develops, it will become more likely that international standards and policies for broader
(65) regulation of human activities that affect ocean ecosystems will be adopted and implemented.

1. According to the passage, until the mid-twentieth century there were few jurisdictional disputes over international waters because

    (A) the nearest coastal nation regulated activities
    (B) few controls or restrictions applied to ocean areas
    (C) the ocean areas were used for only innocent purposes
    (D) the freedom of the seas doctrine settled all claims concerning navigation and fishing
    (E) broad authority over international waters was shared equally among all nations

GO ON TO THE NEXT PAGE.

2. According to the international law doctrines applicable before the mid-twentieth century, if commercial activity within a particular nation's territorial waters threatened all marine life in those waters, the nation would have been

(A) formally censured by an international organization for not properly regulating marine activities
(B) called upon by other nations to establish rules to protect its territorial waters
(C) able but not required to place legal limits on such commercial activities
(D) allowed to resolve the problem at its own discretion providing it could contain the threat to its own territorial waters
(E) permitted to hold the commercial offenders liable only if they were citizens of that particular nation

3. The author suggests that, before the mid-twentieth century, most nations' actions with respect to territorial and international waters indicated that

(A) managing ecosystems in either territorial or international waters was given low priority
(B) unlimited resources in international waters resulted in little interest in territorial waters
(C) nations considered it their responsibility to protect territorial but not international waters
(D) a nation's authority over its citizenry ended at territorial lines
(E) although nations could extend their territorial dominion beyond three miles from their shoreline, most chose not to do so

4. The author cites which one of the following as an effect of the extension of territorial waters beyond the three-mile limit?

(A) increased political pressure on individual nations to establish comprehensive laws regulating ocean resources
(B) a greater number of jurisdictional disputes among nations over the regulation of fishing on the open seas
(C) the opportunity for some nations to manage large ocean ecosystems
(D) a new awareness of the need to minimize pollution caused by navigation
(E) a political incentive for smaller nations to solve the problems of pollution in their coastal waters

5. According to the passage, before the middle of the twentieth century, nations failed to establish rules protecting their territorial waters because

(A) the waters appeared to be unpolluted and to contain unlimited resources
(B) the fishing industry would be adversely affected by such rules
(C) the size of the area that would be subject to such rules was insignificant
(D) the technology needed for pollution control and resource management did not exist
(E) there were few jurisdictional conflicts over nations' territorial waters

6. The passage as a whole can best be described as

(A) a chronology of the events that have led up to a present-day crisis
(B) a legal inquiry into the abuse of existing laws and the likelihood of reform
(C) a political analysis of the problems inherent in directing national attention to an international issue
(D) a historical analysis of a problem that requires international attention
(E) a proposal for adopting and implementing international standards to solve an ecological problem

GO ON TO THE NEXT PAGE.

The human species came into being at the time of the greatest biological diversity in the history of the Earth. Today, as human populations expand and alter the natural environment, they are reducing
(5) biological diversity to its lowest level since the end of the Mesozoic era, 65 million years ago. The ultimate consequences of this biological collision are beyond calculation, but they are certain to be harmful. That, in essence, is the biodiversity crisis.

(10) The history of global diversity can be summarized as follows: after the initial flowering of multicellular animals, there was a swift rise in the number of species in early Paleozoic times (between 600 and 430 million years ago), then plateaulike stagnation
(15) for the remaining 200 million years of the Paleozoic era, and finally a slow but steady climb through the Mesozoic and Cenozoic eras to diversity's all-time high. This history suggests that biological diversity was hard won and a long time in coming.

(20) Furthermore, this pattern of increase was set back by five massive extinction episodes. The most recent of these, during the Cretaceous period, is by far the most famous, because it ended the age of the dinosaurs, conferred hegemony on the mammals, and
(25) ultimately made possible the ascendancy of the human species. But the Cretaceous crisis was minor compared with the Permian extinctions 240 million years ago, during which between 77 and 96 percent of marine animal species perished. It took 5 million
(30) years, well into Mesozoic times, for species diversity to begin a significant recovery.

Within the past 10,000 years biological diversity has entered a wholly new era. Human activity has had a devastating effect on species diversity, and the
(35) rate of human-induced extinctions is accelerating. Half of the bird species of Polynesia have been eliminated through hunting and the destruction of native forests. Hundreds of fish species endemic to Lake Victoria are now threatened with extinction
(40) following the careless introduction of one species of fish, the Nile perch. The list of such biogeographic disasters is extensive.

Because every species is unique and irreplaceable, the loss of biodiversity is the most profound process
(45) of environmental change. Its consequences are also the least predictable because the value of the Earth's biota (the fauna and flora collectively) remains largely unstudied and unappreciated; unlike material and cultural wealth, which we understand because
(50) they are the substance of our everyday lives, biological wealth is usually taken for granted. This is a serious strategic error, one that will be increasingly regretted as time passes. The biota is not only part of a country's heritage, the product of millions of years
(55) of evolution centered on that place; it is also a potential source for immense untapped material wealth in the form of food, medicine, and other commercially important substances.

7. Which one of the following best expresses the main idea of the passage?

(A) The reduction in biodiversity is an irreversible process that represents a setback both for science and for society as a whole.

(B) The material and cultural wealth of a nation are insignificant when compared with the country's biological wealth.

(C) The enormous diversity of life on Earth could not have come about without periodic extinctions that have conferred preeminence on one species at the expense of another.

(D) The human species is in the process of initiating a massive extinction episode that may make past episodes look minor by comparison.

(E) The current decline in species diversity is a human-induced tragedy of incalculable proportions that has potentially grave consequences for the human species.

8. Which one of the following situations is most analogous to the history of global diversity summarized in lines 10–18 of the passage?

(A) The number of fish in a lake declines abruptly as a result of water pollution, then makes a slow comeback after cleanup efforts and the passage of ordinances against dumping.

(B) The concentration of chlorine in the water supply of a large city fluctuates widely before stabilizing at a constant and safe level.

(C) An old-fashioned article of clothing goes in and out of style periodically as a result of features in fashion magazines and the popularity of certain period films.

(D) After valuable mineral deposits are discovered, the population of a geographic region booms, then levels off and begins to decrease at a slow and steady rate.

(E) The variety of styles stocked by a shoe store increases rapidly after the store opens, holds constant for many months, and then gradually creeps upward.

GO ON TO THE NEXT PAGE.

9. The author suggests which one of the following about the Cretaceous crisis?

(A) It was the second most devastating extinction episode in history.

(B) It was the most devastating extinction episode up until that time.

(C) It was less devastating to species diversity than is the current biodiversity crisis.

(D) The rate of extinction among marine animal species as a result of the crisis did not approach 77 percent.

(E) The dinosaurs comprised the great majority of species that perished during the crisis.

10. The author mentions the Nile perch in order to provide an example of

(A) a species that has become extinct through human activity

(B) the typical lack of foresight that has led to biogeographic disaster

(C) a marine animal species that survived the Permian extinctions

(D) a species that is a potential source of material wealth

(E) the kind of action that is necessary to reverse the decline in species diversity

11. All of the following are explicitly mentioned in the passage as contributing to the extinction of species EXCEPT

(A) hunting

(B) pollution

(C) deforestation

(D) the growth of human populations

(E) human-engineered changes in the environment

12. The passage suggests which one of the following about material and cultural wealth?

(A) Because we can readily assess the value of material and cultural wealth, we tend not to take them for granted.

(B) Just as the biota is a source of potential material wealth, it is an untapped source of cultural wealth as well.

(C) Some degree of material and cultural wealth may have to be sacrificed if we are to protect our biological heritage.

(D) Material and cultural wealth are of less value than biological wealth because they have evolved over a shorter period of time.

(E) Material wealth and biological wealth are interdependent in a way that material wealth and cultural wealth are not.

13. The author would be most likely to agree with which one of the following statements about the consequences of the biodiversity crisis?

(A) The loss of species diversity will have as immediate an impact on the material wealth of nations as on their biological wealth.

(B) The crisis will likely end the hegemony of the human race and bring about the ascendancy of another species.

(C) The effects of the loss of species diversity will be dire, but we cannot yet tell how dire.

(D) It is more fruitful to discuss the consequences of the crisis in terms of the potential loss to humanity than in strictly biological terms.

(E) The consequences of the crisis can be minimized, but the pace of extinctions cannot be reversed.

GO ON TO THE NEXT PAGE.

Women's participation in the revolutionary events in France between 1789 and 1795 has only recently been given nuanced treatment. Early twentieth-century historians of the French Revolution are
(5) typified by Jaurès, who, though sympathetic to the women's movement of his own time, never even mentions its antecedents in revolutionary France. Even today most general histories treat only cursorily a few individual women, like Marie Antoinette. The
(10) recent studies by Landes, Badinter, Godineau, and Roudinesco, however, should signal a much-needed reassessment of women's participation.

Godineau and Roudinesco point to three significant phases in that participation. The first, up
(15) to mid-1792, involved those women who wrote political tracts. Typical of their orientation to theoretical issues—in Godineau's view, without practical effect—is Marie Gouze's *Declaration of the Rights of Women.* The emergence of vocal middle-
(20) class women's political clubs marks the second phase. Formed in 1791 as adjuncts of middle-class male political clubs, and originally philanthropic in function, by late 1792 independent clubs of women began to advocate military participation for women.
(25) In the final phase, the famine of 1795 occasioned a mass women's movement: women seized food supplies, held officials hostage, and argued for the implementation of democratic politics. This phase ended in May of 1795 with the military suppression
(30) of this multiclass movement. In all three phases women's participation in politics contrasted markedly with their participation before 1789. Before that date some noblewomen participated indirectly in elections, but such participation by more
(35) than a narrow range of the population—women or men—came only with the Revolution.

What makes the recent studies particularly compelling, however, is not so much their organization of chronology as their unflinching
(40) willingness to confront the reasons for the collapse of the women's movement. For Landes and Badinter, the necessity of women's having to speak in the established vocabularies of certain intellectual and political traditions diminished the ability of the
(45) women's movement to resist suppression. Many women, and many men, they argue, located their vision within the confining tradition of Jean-Jacques Rousseau, who linked male and female roles with public and private spheres respectively. But, when
(50) women went on to make political alliances with radical Jacobin men, Badinter asserts, they adopted a vocabulary and a violently extremist viewpoint that unfortunately was even more damaging to their political interests.
(55) Each of these scholars has a different political agenda and takes a different approach—Godineau, for example, works with police archives while Roudinesco uses explanatory schema from modern psychology. Yet, admirably, each gives center stage
(60) to a group that previously has been marginalized, or

at best undifferentiated, by historians. And in the case of Landes and Badinter, the reader is left with a sobering awareness of the cost to the women of the Revolution of speaking in borrowed voices.

14. Which one of the following best states the main point of the passage?

(A) According to recent historical studies, the participation of women in the revolutionary events of 1789–1795 can most profitably be viewed in three successive stages.

(B) The findings of certain recent historical studies have resulted from an earlier general reassessment, by historians, of women's participation in the revolutionary events of 1789–1795.

(C) Adopting the vocabulary and viewpoint of certain intellectual and political traditions resulted in no political advantage for women in France in the years 1789–1795.

(D) Certain recent historical studies have provided a much-needed description and evaluation of the evolving roles of women in the revolutionary events of 1789–1795.

(E) Historical studies that seek to explain the limitations of the women's movement in France during the years 1789–1795 are much more convincing than are those that seek only to describe the general features of that movement.

GO ON TO THE NEXT PAGE.

15. The passage suggests that Godineau would be likely to agree with which one of the following statements about Marie Gouze's *Declaration of the Rights of Women*?

    (A)   This work was not understood by many of Gouze's contemporaries.
    (B)   This work indirectly inspired the formation of independent women's political clubs.
    (C)   This work had little impact on the world of political action.
    (D)   This work was the most compelling produced by a French woman between 1789 and 1792.
    (E)   This work is typical of the kind of writing French women produced between 1793 and 1795.

16. According to the passage, which one of the following is a true statement about the purpose of the women's political clubs mentioned in line 20?

    (A)   These clubs fostered a mass women's movement.
    (B)   These clubs eventually developed a purpose different from their original purpose.
    (C)   These clubs were founded to advocate military participation for women.
    (D)   These clubs counteracted the original purpose of male political clubs.
    (E)   These clubs lost their direction by the time of the famine of 1795.

17. The primary function of the first paragraph of the passage is to

    (A)   outline the author's argument about women's roles in France between 1789 and 1795
    (B)   anticipate possible challenges to the findings of the recent studies of women in France between 1789 and 1795
    (C)   summarize some long-standing explanations of the role of individual women in France between 1789 and 1795
    (D)   present a context for the discussion of recent studies of women in France between 1789 and 1795
    (E)   characterize various eighteenth-century studies of women in France

18. The passage suggests that Landes and Badinter would be likely to agree with which one of the following statements about the women's movement in France in the 1790s?

    (A)   The movement might have been more successful if women had developed their own political vocabularies.
    (B)   The downfall of the movement was probably unrelated to its alliance with Jacobin men.
    (C)   The movement had a great deal of choice about whether to adopt a Rousseauist political vocabulary.
    (D)   The movement would have triumphed if it had not been suppressed by military means.
    (E)   The movement viewed a Rousseauist political tradition, rather than a Jacobin political ideology, as detrimental to its interests.

19. In the context of the passage, the word "cost" in line 63 refers to the

    (A)   dichotomy of private roles for women and public roles for men
    (B)   almost nonexistent political participation of women before 1789
    (C)   historians' lack of differentiation among various groups of women
    (D)   political alliances women made with radical Jacobin men
    (E)   collapse of the women's movement in the 1790s

20. The author of the passage is primarily concerned with

    (A)   criticizing certain political and intellectual traditions
    (B)   summarizing the main points of several recent historical studies and assessing their value
    (C)   establishing a chronological sequence and arguing for its importance
    (D)   comparing and contrasting women's political activities before and after the French Revolution
    (E)   reexamining a long-held point of view and isolating its strengths and weaknesses

GO ON TO THE NEXT PAGE.

Art historians' approach to French Impressionism has changed significantly in recent years. While a decade ago Rewald's *History of Impressionism,* which emphasizes Impressionist painters' stylistic
(5) innovations, was unchallenged, the literature on Impressionism has now become a kind of ideological battlefield, in which more attention is paid to the subject matter of the paintings, and to the social and moral issues raised by it, than to their style.
(10) Recently, politically charged discussions that address the Impressionists' unequal treatment of men and women and the exclusion of modern industry and labor from their pictures have tended to crowd out the stylistic analysis favored by Rewald and his
(15) followers. In a new work illustrating this trend, Robert L. Herbert dissociates himself from formalists whose preoccupation with the stylistic features of Impressionist painting has, in Herbert's view, left the history out of art history; his aim is to
(20) restore Impressionist paintings "to their sociocultural context." However, his arguments are not, finally, persuasive.

In attempting to place Impressionist painting in its proper historical context, Herbert has redrawn the
(25) traditional boundaries of Impressionism. Limiting himself to the two decades between 1860 and 1880, he assembles under the Impressionist banner what can only be described as a somewhat eccentric grouping of painters. Cézanne, Pisarro, and Sisley
(30) are almost entirely ignored, largely because their paintings do not suit Herbert's emphasis on themes of urban life and suburban leisure, while Manet, Degas, and Caillebotte—who paint scenes of urban life but whom many would hardly characterize as
(35) Impressionists—dominate the first half of the book. Although this new description of Impressionist painting provides a more unified conception of nineteenth-century French painting by grouping quite disparate modernist painters together and
(40) emphasizing their common concerns rather than their stylistic differences, it also forces Herbert to overlook some of the most important genres of Impressionist painting—portraiture, pure landscape, and still-life painting.
(45) Moreover, the rationale for Herbert's emphasis on the social and political realities that Impressionist paintings can be said to communicate rather than on their style is finally undermined by what even Herbert concedes was the failure of Impressionist
(50) painters to serve as particularly conscientious illustrators of their social milieu. They left much ordinary experience—work and poverty, for example—out of their paintings, and what they did put in was transformed by a style that had only an
(55) indirect relationship to the social realities of the world they depicted. Not only were their pictures inventions rather than photographs, they were inventions in which style to some degree disrupted description. Their paintings in effect have two levels
(60) of "subject": what is represented and how it is represented, and no art historian can afford to emphasize one at the expense of the other.

21. Which one of the following best expresses the main point of the passage?

(A) The style of Impressionist paintings has only an indirect relation to their subject matter.
(B) The approach to Impressionism that is illustrated by Herbert's recent book is inadequate.
(C) The historical context of Impressionist paintings is not relevant to their interpretation.
(D) Impressionism emerged from a historical context of ideological conflict and change.
(E) Any adequate future interpretation of Impressionism will have to come to terms with Herbert's view of this art movement.

22. According to the passage, Rewald's book on Impressionism was characterized by which one of the following?

(A) evenhanded objectivity about the achievements of Impressionism
(B) bias in favor of certain Impressionist painters
(C) an emphasis on the stylistic features of Impressionist painting
(D) an idiosyncratic view of which painters were to be classified as Impressionists
(E) a refusal to enter into the ideological debates that had characterized earlier discussions of Impressionism

23. The author implies that Herbert's redefinition of the boundaries of Impressionism resulted from which one of the following?

(A) an exclusive emphasis on form and style
(B) a bias in favor of the representation of modern industry
(C) an attempt to place Impressionism within a specific sociocultural context
(D) a broadening of the term "Impressionism" to include all of nineteenth-century French painting
(E) an insufficient familiarity with earlier interpretations of Impressionism

24. The author states which one of the following about modern industry and labor as subjects for painting?

(A) The Impressionists neglected these subjects in their paintings.
(B) Herbert's book on Impressionism fails to give adequate treatment of these subjects.
(C) The Impressionists' treatment of these subjects was idealized.
(D) Rewald's treatment of Impressionist painters focused inordinately on their representations of these subjects.
(E) Modernist painters presented a distorted picture of these subjects.

GO ON TO THE NEXT PAGE.

25. Which one of the following most accurately describes the structure of the author's argument in the passage?

   (A) The first two paragraphs each present independent arguments for a conclusion that is drawn in the third paragraph.
   (B) A thesis is stated in the first paragraph and revised in the second paragraph, and the revised thesis is supported with an argument in the third paragraph.
   (C) The first two paragraphs discuss and criticize a thesis, and the third paragraph presents an alternative thesis.
   (D) A claim is made in the first paragraph, and the next two paragraphs each present reasons for accepting that claim.
   (E) An argument is presented in the first paragraph, a counterargument is presented in the second paragraph, and the third paragraph suggests a way to resolve the dispute.

26. The author's statement that Impressionist paintings "were inventions in which style to some degree disrupted description" (lines 57–59) serves to

   (A) strengthen the claim that Impressionists sought to emphasize the differences between painting and photography
   (B) weaken the argument that style is the only important feature of Impressionist paintings
   (C) indicate that Impressionists recognized that they had been strongly influenced by photography
   (D) support the argument that an exclusive emphasis on the Impressionists' subject matter is mistaken
   (E) undermine the claim that Impressionists neglected certain kinds of subject matter

27. The author would most likely regard a book on the Impressionists that focused entirely on their style as

   (A) a product of the recent confusion caused by Herbert's book on Impressionism
   (B) emphasizing what Impressionists themselves took to be their primary artistic concern
   (C) an overreaction against the traditional interpretation of Impressionism
   (D) neglecting the most innovative aspects of Impressionism
   (E) addressing only part of what an adequate treatment should cover

S T O P

IF YOU FINISH BEFORE TIME IS CALLED, YOU MAY CHECK YOUR WORK ON THIS SECTION ONLY.
DO NOT WORK ON ANY OTHER SECTION IN THE TEST.

SECTION III

Time—35 minutes

24 Questions

Directions: Each group of questions in this section is based on a set of conditions. In answering some of the questions, it may be useful to draw a rough diagram. Choose the response that most accurately and completely answers each question and blacken the corresponding space on your answer sheet.

Questions 1–6

A law firm has exactly nine partners: Fox, Glassen, Hae, Inman, Jacoby, Kohn, Lopez, Malloy, and Nassar.
　　Kohn's salary is greater than both Inman's and Lopez's.
　　Lopez's salary is greater than Nassar's.
　　Inman's salary is greater than Fox's.
　　Fox's salary is greater than Malloy's.
　　Malloy's salary is greater than Glassen's.
　　Glassen's salary is greater than Jacoby's.
　　Jacoby's salary is greater than Hae's.

1. Which one of the following partners cannot have the third highest salary?

    (A) Fox
    (B) Inman
    (C) Lopez
    (D) Malloy
    (E) Nassar

2. If Malloy and Nassar earn the same salary, at least how many of the partners must have lower salaries than Lopez?

    (A) 3
    (B) 4
    (C) 5
    (D) 6
    (E) 7

3. The salary rankings of each of the nine partners could be completely determined if which one of the following statements were true?

    (A) Lopez's salary is greater than Fox's.
    (B) Lopez's salary is greater than Inman's.
    (C) Nassar's salary is greater than Fox's.
    (D) Nassar's salary is greater than Inman's.
    (E) Nassar's salary is greater than Malloy's.

4. If Nassar's salary is the same as that of one other partner of the firm, which one of the following must be false?

    (A) Inman's salary is less than Lopez's.
    (B) Jacoby's salary is less than Lopez's.
    (C) Lopez's salary is less than Fox's.
    (D) Lopez's salary is less than Hae's.
    (E) Nassar's salary is less than Glassen's.

5. What is the minimum number of different salaries earned by the nine partners of the firm?

    (A) 5
    (B) 6
    (C) 7
    (D) 8
    (E) 9

6. Assume that the partners of the firm are ranked according to their salaries, from first (highest) to ninth (lowest), and that no two salaries are the same. Which one of the following is a complete and accurate list of Glassen's possible ranks?

    (A) fifth
    (B) fifth, sixth
    (C) fifth, seventh
    (D) fifth, sixth, seventh
    (E) fifth, sixth, seventh, eighth

GO ON TO THE NEXT PAGE.

<u>Questions 7–11</u>

Each of five illnesses—J, K, L, M, and N—is characterized by at least one of the following three symptoms: fever, headache, and sneezing. None of the illnesses has any symptom that is not one of these three.

    Illness J is characterized by headache and sneezing.
    Illnesses J and K have no symptoms in common.
    Illnesses J and L have at least one symptom in common.
    Illness L has a greater number of symptoms than illness K.
    Illnesses L and N have no symptoms in common.
    Illness M has more symptoms than illness J.

7.   Which one of the following statements must be false?

    (A)   Illness J has exactly two symptoms.
    (B)   Illness K has exactly one symptom.
    (C)   Illness L has exactly two symptoms.
    (D)   Illness M has exactly three symptoms.
    (E)   Illness N has exactly two symptoms.

8.   In which one of the following pairs could the first member of the pair be characterized by exactly the same number and types of symptoms as the second member of the pair?

    (A)   J and N
    (B)   K and L
    (C)   K and N
    (D)   L and M
    (E)   M and N

9.   If illness L is characterized by a combination of symptoms different from any of the other illnesses, then which one of the following statements must be true?

    (A)   Fever is a symptom of illness L.
    (B)   Sneezing is a symptom of illness L.
    (C)   Headache is a symptom of illness L.
    (D)   Illnesses K and N are characterized by exactly the same symptoms.
    (E)   Illnesses M and N are characterized by exactly the same symptoms.

10.   The illnesses in which one of the following pairs must have exactly one symptom in common?

    (A)   J and L
    (B)   J and M
    (C)   J and N
    (D)   K and L
    (E)   M and N

11.   If Walter has exactly two of the three symptoms, then he cannot have all of the symptoms of

    (A)   both illness J and illness L
    (B)   both illness J and illness N
    (C)   both illness K and illness L
    (D)   both illness K and illness N
    (E)   both illness L and illness N

GO ON TO THE NEXT PAGE.

Questions 12–17

A street cleaning crew works only Monday to Friday, and only during the day. It takes the crew an entire morning or an entire afternoon to clean a street. During one week the crew cleaned exactly eight streets—First, Second, Third, Fourth, Fifth, Sixth, Seventh, and Eighth streets. The following is known about the crew's schedule for the week:

The crew cleaned no street on Friday morning.
The crew cleaned no street on Wednesday afternoon.
It cleaned Fourth Street on Tuesday morning.
It cleaned Seventh Street on Thursday morning.
It cleaned Fourth Street before Sixth Street and after Eighth Street.
It cleaned Second, Fifth, and Eighth streets on afternoons.

12. If the crew cleaned Second Street earlier in the week than Seventh Street, then it must have cleaned which one of the following streets on Tuesday afternoon?

   (A)   First Street
   (B)   Second Street
   (C)   Third Street
   (D)   Fifth Street
   (E)   Eighth Street

13. If the crew cleaned Sixth Street on a morning and cleaned Second Street before Seventh Street, then what is the maximum number of streets whose cleaning times cannot be determined?

   (A)   1
   (B)   2
   (C)   3
   (D)   4
   (E)   5

14. What is the maximum possible number of streets any one of which could be the one the crew cleaned on Friday afternoon?

   (A)   1
   (B)   2
   (C)   3
   (D)   4
   (E)   5

15. If the crew cleaned First Street earlier in the week than Third Street, then which one of the following statements must be false?

   (A)   The crew cleaned First Street on Tuesday afternoon.
   (B)   The crew cleaned Second Street on Thursday afternoon.
   (C)   The crew cleaned Third Street on Wednesday morning.
   (D)   The crew cleaned Fifth Street on Thursday afternoon.
   (E)   The crew cleaned Sixth Street on Friday afternoon.

16. If the crew cleaned Fifth, Sixth, and Seventh streets in numerical order, then what is the maximum number of different schedules any one of which the crew could have had for the entire week?

   (A)   1
   (B)   2
   (C)   3
   (D)   4
   (E)   5

17. Suppose the crew had cleaned Fourth Street on Tuesday afternoon instead of on Tuesday morning, but all other conditions remained the same. Which one of the following statements could be false?

   (A)   The crew cleaned First Street before Second Street.
   (B)   The crew cleaned Second Street before Fifth Street.
   (C)   The crew cleaned Third Street before Second Street.
   (D)   The crew cleaned Sixth Street before Fifth Street.
   (E)   The crew cleaned Seventh Street before Second Street.

GO ON TO THE NEXT PAGE.

Questions 18–24

J, K, L, M, N, and O are square ski chalets of the same size, which are positioned in two straight rows as shown below:

```
         J   K   L
row 1:   ■   ■   ■

row 2:   ■   ■   ■
         M   N   O
```

J is directly opposite M; K is directly opposite N; and L is directly opposite O. After a snowstorm, residents shovel a single continuous path that connects all of the chalets and meets the following conditions:

The path is composed of five straight segments, each of which directly connects exactly two of the chalets.
Each chalet is directly connected by a segment of the path to another chalet.
No chalet is directly connected by segments of the path to more than two other chalets.
No segment of the path crosses any other segment.
One segment of the path directly connects chalets J and N, and another segment directly connects chalets K and L.

18. Which one of the following statements could be true?

(A) One segment of the path directly connects chalets M and K.
(B) One segment of the path directly connects chalets M and L.
(C) One segment of the path directly connects chalets M and O.
(D) One segment of the path directly connects chalets J and K and another segment directly connects chalets K and M.
(E) One segment of the path directly connects chalets O and L and another segment directly connects chalets O and N.

19. If one segment of the path directly connects chalets K and N, then the two chalets in which one of the following pairs must be directly connected to each other by a segment?

(A) J and K
(B) K and O
(C) L and O
(D) M and N
(E) N and O

20. If a segment of the path directly connects chalets J and K, then the two chalets in which one of the following pairs must be directly connected to each other by a segment?

(A) J and M
(B) K and N
(C) K and O
(D) L and O
(E) N and O

21. If one segment of the path directly connects chalets K and O, then which one of the following statements could be true?

(A) Chalet J is directly connected to chalet M.
(B) Chalet K is directly connected to chalet N.
(C) Chalet L is directly connected to chalet O.
(D) Chalet L is directly connected to exactly two chalets.
(E) Chalet O is directly connected to exactly one chalet.

22. Which one of the following statements, if true, guarantees that one segment of the path directly connects chalets M and N?

(A) One segment of the path directly connects chalets K and J.
(B) One segment of the path directly connects chalets N and O.
(C) One segment of the path directly connects chalet K and a chalet in row 2.
(D) One segment of the path directly connects chalet L and a chalet in row 2.
(E) One segment of the path directly connects chalet O and a chalet in row 1.

23. Which one of the following chalets cannot be directly connected by segments of the path to exactly two other chalets?

(A) K
(B) L
(C) M
(D) N
(E) O

24. If no segment of the path directly connects any chalet in row 1 with the chalet in row 2 that is directly opposite it, then each of the following statements must be true EXCEPT:

(A) A segment of the path directly connects chalets M and N.
(B) A segment of the path directly connects chalets N and O.
(C) Chalet L is directly connected to exactly one other chalet.
(D) Chalet N is directly connected to exactly two other chalets.
(E) Chalet O is directly connected to exactly two other chalets.

S T O P

IF YOU FINISH BEFORE TIME IS CALLED, YOU MAY CHECK YOUR WORK ON THIS SECTION ONLY.
DO NOT WORK ON ANY OTHER SECTION IN THE TEST.

SECTION IV

Time—35 minutes

25 Questions

Directions: The questions in this section are based on the reasoning contained in brief statements or passages. For some questions, more than one of the choices could conceivably answer the question. However, you are to choose the best answer; that is, the response that most accurately and completely answers the question. You should not make assumptions that are by commonsense standards implausible, superfluous, or incompatible with the passage. After you have chosen the best answer, blacken the corresponding space on your answer sheet.

1. With the passage of the new tax reform laws, the annual tax burden on low-income taxpayers will be reduced, on average, by anywhere from $100 to $300. Clearly, tax reform is in the interest of low-income taxpayers.

    Which one of the following, if true, most undermines the conclusion above?

    (A) Tax reform, by simplifying the tax code, will save many people the expense of having an accountant do their taxes.

    (B) Tax reform, by eliminating tax incentives to build rental housing, will push up rents an average of about $40 per month for low-income taxpayers.

    (C) Low-income taxpayers have consistently voted for those political candidates who are strong advocates of tax reform.

    (D) The new tax reform laws will permit low- and middle-income taxpayers to deduct child-care expenses from their taxes.

    (E) Under the new tax reform laws, many low-income taxpayers who now pay taxes will no longer be required to do so.

2. If we are to expand the exploration of our solar system, our next manned flight should be to Phobos, one of Mars's moons, rather than to Mars itself. The flight times to each are the same, but the Phobos expedition would require less than half the fuel load of a Mars expedition and would, therefore, be much less costly. So, it is clear that Phobos should be our next step in space exploration.

    Which one of the following, if true, would most help to explain the difference in fuel requirements?

    (A) More equipment would be required to explore Phobos than to explore Mars.

    (B) Smaller spaceships require less fuel than larger spaceships.

    (C) Information learned during the trip to Phobos can be used during a subsequent trip to Mars.

    (D) The shortest distance between Phobos and Mars is less than half the shortest distance between Earth and Mars.

    (E) Lift-off for the return trip from Phobos requires much less fuel than that from Mars because of Phobos' weaker gravitational pull.

3. Scientific research that involves international collaboration has produced papers of greater influence, as measured by the number of times a paper is cited in subsequent papers, than has research without any collaboration. Papers that result from international collaboration are cited an average of seven times, whereas papers with single authors are cited only three times on average. This difference shows that research projects conducted by international research teams are of greater importance than those conducted by single researchers.

    Which one of the following is an assumption on which the argument depends?

    (A) Prolific writers can inflate the number of citations they receive by citing themselves in subsequent papers.

    (B) It is possible to ascertain whether or not a paper is the product of international collaboration by determining the number of citations it has received.

    (C) The number of citations a paper receives is a measure of the importance of the research it reports.

    (D) The collaborative efforts of scientists who are citizens of the same country do not produce papers that are as important as papers that are produced by international collaboration.

    (E) International research teams tend to be more generously funded than are single researchers.

GO ON TO THE NEXT PAGE.

4. It is more desirable to have some form of socialized medicine than a system of medical care relying on the private sector. Socialized medicine is more broadly accessible than is a private-sector system. In addition, since countries with socialized medicine have a lower infant mortality rate than do countries with a system relying entirely on the private sector, socialized medicine seems to be technologically superior.

Which one of the following best indicates a flaw in the argument about the technological superiority of socialized medicine?

(A) The lower infant mortality rate might be due to the system's allowing greater access to medical care.
(B) There is no necessary connection between the economic system of socialism and technological achievement.
(C) Infant mortality is a reliable indicator of the quality of medical care for children.
(D) No list is presented of the countries whose infant mortality statistics are summarized under the two categories, "socialized" and "private-sector."
(E) The argument presupposes the desirability of socialized medicine, which is what the argument seeks to establish.

5. Most parents who are generous are good parents, but some self-centered parents are also good parents. Yet all good parents share one characteristic: they are good listeners.

If all of the statements in the passage are true, which one of the following must also be true?

(A) All parents who are good listeners are good parents.
(B) Some parents who are good listeners are not good parents.
(C) Most parents who are good listeners are generous.
(D) Some parents who are good listeners are self-centered.
(E) Fewer self-centered parents than generous parents are good listeners.

6. Lourdes: Dietary fiber is an important part of a healthful diet. Experts recommend that adults consume 20 to 35 grams of fiber a day.
   Kyra: But a daily intake of fiber that is significantly above that recommended level interferes with mineral absorption, especially the absorption of calcium. The public should be told to cut back on fiber intake.

Which one of the following, if true, most undermines Kyra's recommendation?

(A) Among adults, the average consumption of dietary fiber is at present approximately 10 grams a day.
(B) The more a food is processed, the more the fiber is broken down and the lower the fiber content.
(C) Many foodstuffs that are excellent sources of fiber are economical and readily available.
(D) Adequate calcium intake helps prevent the decrease in bone mass known as osteoporosis.
(E) Many foodstuffs that are excellent sources of fiber are popular with consumers.

7. A certain retailer promotes merchandise by using the following policy:

At all times there is either a "manager's sale" or a "holiday sale" or both going on. All sales are run for exactly one calendar month. In any given month, if a manager wishes to clear out a particular line of merchandise, then a manager's sale is declared. If a holiday falls within the calendar month and there is excess merchandise in the warehouse, then a holiday sale is declared.

However, there is no holiday that falls within the month of August and, in that month, the warehouse never contains excess merchandise.

Which one of the following can be concluded from the passage?

(A) If a holiday falls within a given month and there is no extra merchandise in the warehouse that month, then a holiday sale is declared.
(B) If a holiday sale is not being run, then it is the month of August.
(C) If a manager's sale is being run in some month, then there is no excess merchandise in the warehouse in that month.
(D) If there is not a manager's sale being run in some month, then there is a holiday sale being run in that month.
(E) If there is no excess merchandise in the warehouse, then it is the month of August.

GO ON TO THE NEXT PAGE.

8. Prominent business executives often play active roles in United States presidential campaigns as fund-raisers or backroom strategists, but few actually seek to become president themselves. Throughout history the great majority of those who have sought to become president have been lawyers, military leaders, or full-time politicians. This is understandable, for the personality and skills that make for success in business do not make for success in politics. Business is largely hierarchical, whereas politics is coordinative. As a result, business executives tend to be uncomfortable with compromises and power-sharing, which are inherent in politics.

Which one of the following, if true, most seriously weakens the proposed explanation of why business executives do not run for president?

(A) Many of the most active presidential fund-raisers and backroom strategists are themselves politicians.

(B) Military leaders are generally no more comfortable with compromises and power-sharing than are business executives.

(C) Some of the skills needed to become a successful lawyer are different from some of those needed to become a successful military leader.

(D) Some former presidents have engaged in business ventures after leaving office.

(E) Some hierarchically structured companies have been major financial supporters of candidates for president.

9. A scientific theory is a good theory if it satisfies two requirements: It must accurately describe a large class of observations in terms of a model that is simple enough to contain only a few elements, and it must make definite predictions about the results of future observations. For example, Aristotle's cosmological theory, which claimed that everything was made out of four elements—earth, air, fire, and water—satisfied the first requirement, but it did not make any definite predictions. Thus, Aristotle's cosmological theory was not a good theory.

If all the statements in the passage are true, each of the following must also be true EXCEPT:

(A) Prediction about the results of future observations must be made by any good scientific theory.

(B) Observation of physical phenomena was not a major concern in Aristotle's cosmological theory.

(C) Four elements can be the basis of a scientific model that is simple enough to meet the simplicity criterion of a good theory.

(D) A scientific model that contains many elements is not a good theory.

(E) Aristotle's cosmological theory described a large class of observations in terms of only four elements.

10. Millions of irreplaceable exhibits in natural history museums are currently allowed to decay. Yet without analyses of eggs from museums, the studies linking pesticides with the decline of birds of prey would have been impossible. Therefore, funds must be raised to preserve at least those exhibits that will be most valuable to science in the future.

The argument presupposes that

(A) if a museum exhibit is irreplaceable, its preservation is of an importance that overrides economic considerations

(B) the scientific analysis of museum exhibits can be performed in a nondestructive way

(C) eggs of extinct species should be analyzed to increase knowledge of genetic relationships among species

(D) it can be known at this time what data will be of most use to scientific investigators in the future

(E) the decay of organic material in natural history exhibits is natural and cannot be prevented

11. Compared to nonprofit hospitals of the same size, investor-owned hospitals require less public investment in the form of tax breaks, use fewer employees, and have higher occupancy levels. It can therefore be concluded that investor-owned hospitals are a better way of delivering medical care than are nonprofit hospitals.

Which one of the following, if true, most undermines the conclusion drawn above?

(A) Nonprofit hospitals charge more per bed than do investor-owned hospitals.

(B) Patients in nonprofit hospitals recover more quickly than do patients with comparable illnesses in investor-owned hospitals.

(C) Nonprofit hospitals do more fundraising than do investor-owned hospitals.

(D) Doctors at nonprofit hospitals earn higher salaries than do similarly-qualified doctors at investor-owned hospitals.

(E) Nonprofit hospitals receive more donations than do investor-owned hospitals.

GO ON TO THE NEXT PAGE.

12. The ancient Egyptian pharaoh Akhenaten, who had a profound effect during his lifetime on Egyptian art and religion, was well loved and highly respected by his subjects. We know this from the fierce loyalty shown to him by his palace guards, as documented in reports written during Akhenaten's reign.

A questionable technique used in the argument is to

(A) introduce information that actually contradicts the conclusion

(B) rely on evidence that in principle would be impossible to challenge

(C) make a generalization based on a sample that is likely to be unrepresentative

(D) depend on the ambiguity of the term "ancient"

(E) apply present-day standards in an inappropriate way to ancient times

13. Physician: The patient is suffering either from disease X or else from disease Y, but there is no available test for distinguishing X from Y. Therefore, since there is an effective treatment for Y but no treatment for X, we must act on the assumption that the patient has a case of Y.

The physician's reasoning could be based on which one of the following principles?

(A) In treating a patient who has one or the other of two diseases, it is more important to treat the diseases than to determine which of the two diseases the patient has.

(B) If circumstances beyond a decision maker's control will affect the outcome of the decision maker's actions, the decision maker must assume that circumstances are unfavorable.

(C) When the soundness of a strategy depends on the truth of a certain assumption, the first step in putting the strategy into effect must be to test the truth of this assumption.

(D) When success is possible only if a circumstance beyond one's control is favorable, then one's strategy must be based on the assumption that this circumstance is in fact favorable.

(E) When only one strategy carries the possibility of success, circumstances must as much as possible be changed to fit this strategy.

14. Consumer advocate: Tropical oils are high in saturated fats, which increase the risk of heart disease. Fortunately, in most prepared food tropical oils can be replaced by healthier alternatives without noticeably affecting taste. Therefore, intensive publicity about the disadvantage of tropical oils will be likely to result in dietary changes that will diminish many people's risk of developing heart disease.

Nutritionist: The major sources of saturated fat in the average North American diet are meat, poultry, and dairy products, not tropical oils. Thus, focusing attention on the health hazards of tropical oils would be counterproductive, because it would encourage people to believe that more substantial dietary changes are unnecessary.

Which one of the following is a point at issue between the nutritionist and the consumer advocate?

(A) whether a diet that regularly includes large quantities of tropical oil can increase the risk of heart disease

(B) whether intensive publicity campaigns can be effective as a means of changing people's eating habits

(C) whether more people in North America would benefit from reducing the amount of meat they consume than would benefit from eliminating tropical oils from their diets

(D) whether some people's diets could be made significantly healthier if they replaced all tropical oils with vegetable oils that are significantly lower in saturated fat

(E) whether conducting a publicity campaign that, by focusing on the health hazards of tropical oils, persuades people to replace such oils with healthier alternatives is a good public-health strategy

GO ON TO THE NEXT PAGE.

15. People who take what others regard as a ridiculous position should not bother to say, "I mean every word!" For either their position truly is ridiculous, in which case insisting that they are serious about it only exposes them to deeper embarrassment, or else their position has merit, in which case they should meet disbelief with rational argument rather than with assurances of their sincerity.

Which one of the following arguments is most similar in its reasoning to the argument above?

(A) A practice that has been denounced as a poor practice should not be defended on the grounds that "this is how we have always done it." If the practice is a poor one, so much the worse that it has been extensively used; if it is not a poor one, there must be a better reason for engaging in it than inertia.

(B) People who are asked why they eat some of the unusual foods they eat should not answer, "because that is what I like." This sort of answer will sound either naive or evasive and thus will satisfy no one.

(C) People whose taste in clothes is being criticized should not reply, "Every penny I spent on these clothes I earned honestly." For the issue raised by the critics is not how the money was come by but rather whether it was spent wisely.

(D) Scholars who champion unpopular new theories should not assume that the widespread rejection of their ideas shows that they "must be on the right track." The truth is that few theories of any consequence are either wholly right or wholly wrong and thus there is no substitute for patient work in ascertaining which parts are right.

(E) People who set themselves goals that others denounce as overly ambitious do little to silence their critics if they say, "I can accomplish this if anyone can." Rather, those people should either admit that their critics are right or not dignify the criticism with any reply.

16. Concetta: Franchot was a great writer because she was ahead of her time in understanding that industrialization was taking an unconscionable toll on the family structure of the working class.

Alicia: Franchot was not a great writer. The mark of a great writer is the ability to move people with the power of the written word, not the ability to be among the first to grasp a social issue. Besides, the social consequences of industrialization were widely understood in Franchot's day.

In her disagreement with Concetta, Alicia does which one of the following?

(A) accepts Concetta's criterion and then adds evidence to Concetta's case

(B) discredits Concetta's evidence and then generalizes from new evidence

(C) rejects Concetta's criterion and then disputes a specific claim

(D) disputes Concetta's conclusion and then presents facts in support of an alternative criterion

(E) attacks one of Concetta's claims and then criticizes the structure of her argument

GO ON TO THE NEXT PAGE.

Questions 17–18

Zelda: Dr. Ladlow, a research psychologist, has convincingly demonstrated that his theory about the determinants of rat behavior generates consistently accurate predictions about how rats will perform in a maze. On the basis of this evidence, Dr. Ladlow has claimed that his theory is irrefutably correct.

Anson: Then Dr. Ladlow is not a responsible psychologist. Dr. Ladlow's evidence does not conclusively prove that his theory is correct. Responsible psychologists always accept the possibility that new evidence will show that their theories are incorrect.

17. Which one of the following can be properly inferred from Anson's argument?

(A) Dr. Ladlow's evidence that his theory generates consistently accurate predictions about how rats will perform in a maze is inaccurate.

(B) Psychologists who can derive consistently accurate predictions about how rats will perform in a maze from their theories cannot responsibly conclude that those theories cannot be disproved.

(C) No matter how responsible psychologists are, they can never develop correct theoretical explanations.

(D) Responsible psychologists do not make predictions about how rats will perform in a maze.

(E) Psychologists who accept the possibility that new evidence will show that their theories are incorrect are responsible psychologists.

18. Anson bases his conclusion about Dr. Ladlow on which one of the following?

(A) an attack on Dr. Ladlow's character
(B) the application of a general principle
(C) the use of an ambiguous term
(D) the discrediting of facts
(E) the rejection of a theoretical explanation

19. Smith: Meat in the diet *is* healthy, despite what some people say. After all, most doctors do eat meat, and who knows more about health than doctors do?

Which one of the following is a flaw in Smith's reasoning?

(A) attacking the opponents' motives instead of their argument
(B) generalizing on the basis of a sample consisting of atypical cases
(C) assuming at the outset what the argument claims to establish through reasoning
(D) appealing to authority, even when different authorities give conflicting advice about an issue
(E) taking for granted that experts do not act counter to what, according to their expertise, is in their best interest

20. The rise in the prosperity of England subsequent to 1840 can be attributed to the adoption of the policy of free trade, since economic conditions improved only when that policy had been implemented.

The reasoning in the above argument most closely parallels that in which one of the following?

(A) An exhaustive search of the marshes last year revealed no sign of marsh hawks, so it can be assumed that a similar search this year would reveal equally little sign of that kind of bird.

(B) Building a circular bypass road around Plainfield probably helped the flow of local traffic in the town center, since a circular bypass road generally cuts a city's through traffic markedly.

(C) Before the banks raised their interest rates, people on average incomes could almost afford a mortgage for an amount twice their salary, hence the rate increase has now put mortgages beyond their reach.

(D) Since the improvement in the company's profitability began to occur after the vice president's new morale-building program was put in place, that program can be credited with the improved result.

(E) The extinction of the dinosaurs was brought about by an asteroid colliding with Earth, so their extinction could not have come before the collision.

GO ON TO THE NEXT PAGE.

21. During construction of the Quebec Bridge in 1907, the bridge's designer, Theodore Cooper, received word that the suspended span being built out from the bridge's cantilever was deflecting downward by a fraction of an inch. Before he could telegraph to freeze the project, the whole cantilever arm broke off and plunged, along with seven dozen workers, into the St. Lawrence River. It was the worst bridge construction disaster in history. As a direct result of the inquiry that followed, the engineering "rules of thumb" by which thousands of bridges had been built went down with the Quebec Bridge. Twentieth-century bridge engineers would thereafter depend on far more rigorous applications of mathematical analysis.

Which one of the following statements can be properly inferred from the passage?

(A) Bridges built before about 1907 were built without thorough mathematical analysis and, therefore, were unsafe for the public to use.
(B) Cooper's absence from the Quebec Bridge construction site resulted in the breaking off of the cantilever.
(C) Nineteenth-century bridge engineers relied on their rules of thumb because analytical methods were inadequate to solve their design problems.
(D) Only a more rigorous application of mathematical analysis to the design of the Quebec Bridge could have prevented its collapse.
(E) Prior to 1907 the mathematical analysis incorporated in engineering rules of thumb was insufficient to completely assure the safety of bridges under construction.

22. Most children find it very difficult to explain exactly what the words they use mean when those words do not refer to things that can be seen or touched. Yet, since children are able to use these words to convey the feelings and emotions they are obviously experiencing, understanding what a word means clearly does not depend on being able to explain it.

Which one of the following principles, if accepted, would provide the most justification for the conclusion?

(A) The fact that a task is very difficult for most people does not mean that no one can do it.
(B) Anyone who can provide an exact explanation of a word has a clear understanding of what that word means.
(C) Words that refer to emotions invariably have less narrowly circumscribed conventional meanings than do words that refer to physical objects.
(D) When someone appropriately uses a word to convey something that he or she is experiencing, that person understands what that word means.
(E) Words can be explained satisfactorily only when they refer to things that can be seen or touched.

Questions 23–24

The brains of identical twins are genetically identical. When only one of a pair of identical twins is a schizophrenic, certain areas of the affected twin's brain are smaller than corresponding areas in the brain of the unaffected twin. No such differences are found when neither twin is schizophrenic. Therefore, this discovery provides definitive evidence that schizophrenia is caused by damage to the physical structure of the brain.

23. Which one of the following is an assumption required by the argument?

(A) The brain of a person suffering from schizophrenia is smaller than the brain of anyone not suffering from schizophrenia.
(B) The relative smallness of certain parts of the brains of schizophrenics is not the result of schizophrenia or of medications used in its treatment.
(C) The brain of a person with an identical twin is no smaller, on average, than the brain of a person who is not a twin.
(D) When a pair of identical twins both suffer from schizophrenia, their brains are the same size.
(E) People who have an identical twin are no more likely to suffer from schizophrenia than those who do not.

24. If the statements on which the conclusion above is based are all true, each of the following could be true EXCEPT:

(A) People who lack a genetic susceptibility for the disease will not develop schizophrenia.
(B) Medications can control most of the symptoms of schizophrenia in most patients but will never be able to cure it.
(C) The brains of schizophrenics share many of the characteristics found in those of people without the disorder.
(D) It will eventually be possible to determine whether or not someone will develop schizophrenia on the basis of genetic information alone.
(E) Brain abnormalities associated with schizophrenia are the result of childhood viral infections that inhibit the development of brain cells.

GO ON TO THE NEXT PAGE.

25. Sixty adults were asked to keep a diary of their meals, including what they consumed, when, and in the company of how many people. It was found that at meals with which they drank alcoholic beverages, they consumed about 175 calories more from nonalcoholic sources than they did at meals with which they did not drink alcoholic beverages.

Each of the following, if true, contributes to an explanation of the difference in caloric intake EXCEPT:

(A)   Diners spent a much longer time at meals served with alcohol than they did at those served without alcohol.

(B)   The meals eaten later in the day tended to be larger than those eaten earlier in the day, and later meals were more likely to include alcohol.

(C)   People eat more when there are more people present at the meal, and more people tended to be present at meals served with alcohol than at meals served without alcohol.

(D)   The meals that were most carefully prepared and most attractively served tended to be those at which alcoholic beverages were consumed.

(E)   At meals that included alcohol, relatively more of the total calories consumed came from carbohydrates and relatively fewer of them came from fats and proteins.

S T O P

IF YOU FINISH BEFORE TIME IS CALLED, YOU MAY CHECK YOUR WORK ON THIS SECTION ONLY.
DO NOT WORK ON ANY OTHER SECTION IN THE TEST.

Acknowledgment is made to the following for permission to reprint selections that appear in PrepTest IV:

From "Management of Large Marine Ecosystems: Developing a New Rule of Customary International Law" by Martin H. Belsky. *San Diego Law Review*, Volume 22, 1985. © 1985 by the University of San Diego. Used by permission.

SIGNATURE ——————————————————

DATE

LSAT WRITING SAMPLE TOPIC

Ralston, the capital city, is planning its 200th anniversary celebration, which will end with speeches in front of City Hall. The town is considering including a theatrical performance. Write an argument favoring one of the following two productions over the other, with two considerations guiding your decision:

- The town wants to promote significant out-of-town interest in the event.
- The town wants to encourage as much community participation as possible.

First Lady, a serious drama, was written by a local author who is also a community leader in Ralston. It is the story of Ada Jeffers, the controversial, outspoken wife of the first governor. Jeffers' unceasing, uncompromising stance against various forms of oppression was the subject of a nationally broadcast television special last year. Teri Alan, a native of Ralston and famous film actor, will play the lead. She has promised to recruit a small professional cast to perform the parts of the main characters in the play, and all other roles will be filled by area residents. The town's newspaper, the *Ralston Times Daily*, in conjunction with the town historical society, will publish a special anniversary edition featuring Jeffers' many activities.

Ralston Redux is a musical revue based on a fictionalized account of the colorful life and exploits of Herbert Ralston, the town founder and confidence man. Two of the region's leading satirists adapted the script from a popular play. The show includes a children's chorus and a number of crowd scenes, all to be played by community members. Leading roles will be filled through auditions. The director of a successful summer stock company has offered her assistance and the services of her professional technical crew. The Ralston High School Band, which has won the regional competition for the past three years, will provide the music. Local merchants have contributed money for a fireworks extravaganza that will be part of the play's finale.

Directions:

1. Use the Answer Key on the next page to check your answers.

2. Use the Scoring Worksheet below to compute your raw score.

3. Use the Score Conversion Chart to convert your raw score into the 120-180 scale.

Scoring Worksheet

1. Enter the number of questions you answered correctly in each section.

	Number Correct
SECTION I	_____
SECTION II	_____
SECTION III	_____
SECTION IV	_____

2. Enter the sum here: _____
   This is your Raw Score.

Conversion Chart
Form 2LSS15

For Converting Raw Score to the 120-180 LSAT Scaled Score

Reported Score	Raw Score Lowest	Highest
180	99	100
179	98	98
178	97	97
177	—*	—*
176	96	96
175	95	95
174	94	94
173	93	93
172	92	92
171	91	91
170	90	90
169	88	89
168	87	87
167	86	86
166	84	85
165	83	83
164	81	82
163	79	80
162	78	78
161	76	77
160	74	75
159	72	73
158	70	71
157	68	69
156	66	67
155	64	65
154	63	63
153	61	62
152	59	60
151	57	58
150	55	56
149	53	54
148	51	52
147	49	50
146	47	48
145	45	46
144	44	44
143	42	43
142	40	41
141	38	39
140	37	37
139	35	36
138	34	34
137	32	33
136	31	31
135	29	30
134	28	28
133	27	27
132	25	26
131	24	24
130	23	23
129	22	22
128	21	21
127	20	20
126	19	19
125	—*	—*
124	18	18
123	—*	—*
122	17	17
121	16	16
120	0	15

*There is no raw score that will produce this scaled score for this form.

SECTION I

1.	E	8.	D	15.	D	22.	B
2.	A	9.	A	16.	A	23.	C
3.	E	10.	E	17.	C	24.	E
4.	D	11.	C	18.	D		
5.	C	12.	E	19.	D		
6.	E	13.	D	20.	B		
7.	D	14.	C	21.	B		

SECTION II

1.	B	8.	E	15.	C	22.	C
2.	C	9.	D	16.	B	23.	C
3.	A	10.	B	17.	D	24.	A
4.	C	11.	B	18.	A	25.	D
5.	C	12.	A	19.	E	26.	D
6.	D	13.	C	20.	B	27.	E
7.	E	14.	D	21.	B		

SECTION III

1.	D	8.	C	15.	A	22.	A
2.	C	9.	A	16.	D	23.	C
3.	D	10.	E	17.	B	24.	B
4.	D	11.	E	18.	E		
5.	C	12.	B	19.	C		
6.	D	13.	C	20.	D		
7.	E	14.	E	21.	A		

SECTION IV

1.	B	8.	B	15.	A	22.	D
2.	E	9.	B	16.	C	23.	B
3.	C	10.	D	17.	B	24.	D
4.	A	11.	B	18.	B	25.	E
5.	D	12.	C	19.	E		
6.	A	13.	D	20.	D		
7.	D	14.	E	21.	E		

The Official

LSAT

PrepTest™ V

The sample test that follows consists of four sections corresponding to the four scored sections of the June 1992 LSAT.

June 1992
Form 3LSS16

General Directions for the LSAT Answer Sheet

The actual testing time for this portion of the test will be 2 hours 55 minutes. There are five sections, each with a time limit of 35 minutes. The supervisor will tell you when to begin and end each section. If you finish a section before time is called, you may check your work on that section <u>only</u>; do not turn to any other section of the test book and do not work on any other section either in the test book or on the answer sheet.

There are several different types of questions on the test, and each question type has its own directions. <u>Be sure you understand the directions for each question type before attempting to answer any questions in that section.</u>

Not everyone will finish all the questions in the time allowed. Do not hurry, but work steadily and as quickly as you can without sacrificing accuracy. You are advised to use your time effectively. If a question seems too difficult, go on to the next one and return to the difficult question after completing the section. MARK THE BEST ANSWER YOU CAN FOR EVERY QUESTION. NO DEDUCTIONS WILL BE MADE FOR WRONG ANSWERS. YOUR SCORE WILL BE BASED ONLY ON THE NUMBER OF QUESTIONS YOU ANSWER CORRECTLY.

ALL YOUR ANSWERS MUST BE MARKED ON THE ANSWER SHEET. Answer spaces for each question are lettered to correspond with the letters of the potential answers to each question in the test book. After you have decided which of the answers is correct, blacken the corresponding space on the answer sheet. BE SURE THAT EACH MARK IS BLACK AND COMPLETELY FILLS THE ANSWER SPACE. Give only one answer to each question. If you change an answer, be sure that all previous marks are <u>erased completely</u>. Since the answer sheet is machine scored, incomplete erasures may be interpreted as intended answers. ANSWERS RECORDED IN THE TEST BOOK WILL NOT BE SCORED.

There may be more questions noted on this answer sheet than there are questions in a section. Do not be concerned but be certain that the section and number of the question you are answering matches the answer sheet section and question number. Additional answer spaces in any answer sheet section should be left blank. Begin your next section in the number one answer space for that section.

Score Cancellation

Complete this section only if you are absolutely certain you want to cancel your score. A CANCELLATION REQUEST CANNOT BE RESCINDED. IF YOU ARE AT ALL UNCERTAIN, YOU SHOULD NOT COMPLETE THIS SECTION; INSTEAD, YOU SHOULD USE THE TIME ALLOWED AFTER THE TEST (UP TO 5 DAYS) TO FULLY CONSIDER YOUR DECISION.

To cancel your score from this administration, you must:

A. fill in the ovals here........ ◯ ◯

B. read the following statement. Then sign your name and enter the date.

I certify that I wish to cancel my test score from this administration. I understand that my request is irreversible and that my score will not be sent to me or to the law schools to which I apply.

_____
Sign your name in full

_____
Date

HOW DID YOU PREPARE FOR THE LSAT?
(Select all that apply.)

Responses to this item are voluntary and will be used for statistical research purposes only.

◯ By studying the sample questions in the *LSAT/LSDAS Registration and Information Book.*
◯ By taking the free sample LSAT.
◯ By working through *The Official LSAT PrepTest(s), PrepBook, Workbooks, or PrepKit.*
◯ By using a book on how to prepare for the LSAT **not** published by Law Services.
◯ By attending a commercial test preparation or coaching course.
◯ By attending a test preparation or coaching course offered through an undergraduate institution.
◯ Self study.
◯ Other preparation.
◯ No preparation.

CERTIFYING STATEMENT

Please write (DO NOT PRINT) the following statement. Sign and date.

I certify that I am the examinee whose name appears on this answer sheet and that I am here to take the LSAT for the sole purpose of being considered for admission to law school. I further certify that I will neither assist nor receive assistance from any other candidate, and I agree not to copy or retain examination questions or to transmit them in any form to any other person.

_____
_____
_____
_____
_____
_____
_____
_____
_____
_____

SIGNATURE: _____ TODAY'S DATE: ___/___/___
                                                    MONTH DAY YEAR

INSTRUCTIONS FOR COMPLETING THE BIOGRAPHICAL AREA ARE ON THE BACK COVER OF YOUR TEST BOOKLET.
USE ONLY A NO. 2 OR HB PENCIL TO COMPLETE THIS ANSWER SHEET. DO NOT USE INK.

1 LAST NAME / FIRST NAME / MI

(Grid of bubbles A–Z for each letter position)

2 DATE OF BIRTH

MONTH	DAY	YEAR
○ Jan		
○ Feb		
○ Mar		
○ Apr		
○ May		
○ June		
○ July		
○ Aug		
○ Sept		
○ Oct		
○ Nov		
○ Dec		

(Number bubbles 0–9 for DAY and YEAR)

3 SOCIAL SECURITY NO.

(Number bubbles 0–9)

Right Mark: ●
Wrong Marks: ⊘ ⊗ ⊙

4 ETHNIC DESCRIPTION

- ○ American Indian/ Alaskan Native
- ○ Asian/Pacific Islander
- ○ Black/African Amer.
- ○ Canadian Aboriginal
- ○ Caucasian/White
- ○ Chicano/Mex. Amer.
- ○ Hispanic
- ○ Puerto Rican
- ○ Other

5 GENDER
- ○ Male
- ○ Female

6 DOMINANT LANGUAGE
- ○ English
- ○ Other

7 ENGLISH FLUENCY
- ○ Yes
- ○ No

8 CENTER NUMBER

(Number bubbles 0–9)

9 TEST FORM CODE

(Number bubbles 0–9)

10 TEST BOOK SERIAL NO.

11 TEST FORM

12 TEST DATE

_____ / _____ / _____
MONTH   DAY   YEAR

13 PLEASE PRINT ALL INFORMATION

LAST NAME _____ FIRST _____

MAILING ADDRESS _____

_____

_____

_____

SOCIAL SECURITY/ SOCIAL INSURANCE NO.

═══ LAW SCHOOL ADMISSION TEST ═══

MARK ONE AND ONLY ONE ANSWER TO EACH QUESTION. BE SURE TO FILL IN COMPLETELY THE SPACE FOR YOUR INTENDED ANSWER CHOICE. IF YOU ERASE, DO SO COMPLETELY. MAKE NO STRAY MARKS.

SECTION 1 — items 1–30, each with choices Ⓐ Ⓑ Ⓒ Ⓓ Ⓔ

SECTION 2 — items 1–30, each with choices Ⓐ Ⓑ Ⓒ Ⓓ Ⓔ

SECTION 3 — items 1–30, each with choices Ⓐ Ⓑ Ⓒ Ⓓ Ⓔ

SECTION 4 — items 1–30, each with choices Ⓐ Ⓑ Ⓒ Ⓓ Ⓔ

SECTION 5 — items 1–30, each with choices Ⓐ Ⓑ Ⓒ Ⓓ Ⓔ

NOTE: If you have a new address, you must write Law Services at Box 2000-C, Newtown, PA 18940 or call (215) 968-1001. We cannot guarantee that all address changes will be processed before scores are mailed, so be sure to notify your post office of your forwarding address.

FOR LAW SERVICES USE ONLY

LR	
LW	
LCS	

SECTION I

Time—35 minutes

25 Questions

Directions: The questions in this section are based on the reasoning contained in brief statements or passages. For some questions, more than one of the choices could conceivably answer the question. However, you are to choose the best answer; that is, the response that most accurately and completely answers the question. You should not make assumptions that are by commonsense standards implausible, superfluous, or incompatible with the passage. After you have chosen the best answer, blacken the corresponding space on your answer sheet.

1. Something must be done to ease traffic congestion. In traditional small towns, people used to work and shop in the same town in which they lived; but now that stores and workplaces are located far away from residential areas, people cannot avoid traveling long distances each day. Traffic congestion is so heavy on all roads that, even on major highways where the maximum speed limit is 55 miles per hour, the actual speed averages only 35 miles per hour.

   Which one of the following proposals is most supported by the statements above?

   (A) The maximum speed limit on major highways should be increased.
   (B) People who now travel on major highways should be encouraged to travel on secondary roads instead.
   (C) Residents of the remaining traditional small towns should be encouraged to move to the suburbs.
   (D) Drivers who travel well below the maximum speed limit on major highways should be fined.
   (E) New businesses should be encouraged to locate closer to where their workers would live.

2. College professor: College students do not write nearly as well as they used to. Almost all of the papers that my students have done for me this year have been poorly written and ungrammatical.

   Which one of the following is the most serious weakness in the argument made by the professor?

   (A) It requires confirmation that the change in the professor's students is representative of a change among college students in general.
   (B) It offers no proof to the effect that the professor is an accurate judge of writing ability.
   (C) It does not take into account the possibility that the professor is a poor teacher.
   (D) It fails to present contrary evidence.
   (E) It fails to define its terms sufficiently.

Questions 3–4

Mayor of Plainsville: In order to help the economy of Plainsville, I am using some of our tax revenues to help bring a major highway through the town and thereby attract new business to Plainsville.

Citizens' group: You must have interests other than our economy in mind. If you were really interested in helping our economy, you would instead allocate the revenues to building a new business park, since it would bring in twice the business that your highway would.

3. The argument by the citizens' group relies on which one of the following assumptions?

   (A) Plainsville presently has no major highways running through it.
   (B) The mayor accepts that a new business park would bring in more new business than would the new highway.
   (C) The new highway would have no benefits for Plainsville other than attracting new business.
   (D) The mayor is required to get approval for all tax revenue allocation plans from the city council.
   (E) Plainsville's economy will not be helped unless a new business park of the sort envisioned by the citizens' group is built.

4. Which one of the following principles, if accepted, would most help the citizens' group to justify drawing its conclusion that the mayor has in mind interests other than Plainsville's economy?

   (A) Anyone really pursuing a cause will choose the means that that person believes will advance the cause the farthest.
   (B) Any goal that includes helping the economy of a community will require public revenues in order to be achieved.
   (C) Anyone planning to use resources collected from a group must consult the members of the group before using the resources.
   (D) Any cause worth committing oneself to must include specific goals toward which one can work.
   (E) Any cause not pursued by public officials, if it is to be pursued at all, must be pursued by members of the community.

GO ON TO THE NEXT PAGE.

5. Recently, highly skilled workers in Eastern Europe have left jobs in record numbers to emigrate to the West. It is therefore likely that skilled workers who remain in Eastern Europe are in high demand in their home countries.

Which one of the following, if true, most seriously weakens the argument?

(A) Eastern European factories prefer to hire workers from their home countries rather than to import workers from abroad.

(B) Major changes in Eastern European economic structures have led to the elimination of many positions previously held by the highly skilled emigrants.

(C) Many Eastern European emigrants need to acquire new skills after finding work in the West.

(D) Eastern European countries plan to train many new workers to replace the highly skilled workers who have emigrated.

(E) Because of the departure of skilled workers from Eastern European countries, many positions are now unfilled.

6. Historian: Alexander the Great should not be judged by appeal to current notions of justice. Alexander, an ancient figure of heroic stature, should be judged by the standards of his own culture. That is, did he live up to his culture's ideals of leadership? Did Alexander elevate the contemporary standards of justice? Was he, in his day, judged to be a just and wise ruler?

Student: But you cannot tell whether or not Alexander raised the contemporary standards of justice without invoking standards other than those of his own culture.

Which one of the following argumentative strategies does the student use in responding to the historian?

(A) arguing that applying the historian's principle would require a knowledge of the past that is necessarily inaccessible to current scholarship

(B) attempting to undermine the historian's principle by showing that some of its consequences are inconsistent with each other

(C) showing that the principle the historian invokes, when applied to Alexander, does not justify the assertion that he was heroic

(D) questioning the historian's motivation for determining whether a standard of behavior has been raised or lowered

(E) claiming that one of the historian's criteria for judging Alexander is inconsistent with the principle that the historian has advanced

Questions 7–8

Two paleontologists, Dr. Tyson and Dr. Rees, disagree over the interpretation of certain footprints that were left among other footprints in hardened volcanic ash at site G. Dr. Tyson claims they are clearly early hominid footprints since they show human characteristics: a squarish heel and a big toe immediately adjacent to the next toe. However, since the footprints indicate that if hominids made those prints they would have had to walk in an unexpected cross-stepping manner, by placing the left foot to the right of the right foot, Dr. Rees rejects Dr. Tyson's conclusion.

7. The disagreement between the two paleontologists is over which one of the following?

(A) the relative significance of various aspects of the evidence

(B) the assumption that early hominid footprints are distinguishable from other footprints

(C) the possibility of using the evidence of footprints to determine the gait of the creature that made those footprints

(D) the assumption that evidence from one paleontologic site is enough to support a conclusion

(E) the likelihood that early hominids would have walked upright on two feet

8. Which one of the following, if true, most seriously undermines Dr. Tyson's conclusion?

(A) The footprints showing human characteristics were clearly those of at least two distinct individuals.

(B) Certain species of bears had feet very like human feet, except that the outside toe on each foot was the biggest toe and the innermost toe was the smallest toe.

(C) Footprints shaped like a human's that do not show a cross-stepping pattern exist at site M, which is a mile away from site G, and the two sets of footprints are contemporaneous.

(D) When the moist volcanic ash became sealed under additional layers of ash before hardening, some details of some of the footprints were erased.

(E) Most of the other footprints at site G were of animals with hooves.

GO ON TO THE NEXT PAGE.

9. It is not known whether bovine spongiform encephalopathy (BSE), a disease of cattle invariably deadly to them, can be transmitted directly from one infected animal to another at all stages of the infection. If it can be, there is now a reservoir of infected cattle incubating the disease. There are no diagnostic tests to identify infected animals before the animals show overt symptoms. Therefore, if such direct transmission occurs, the disease cannot be eradicated by _____.

Which one of the following best completes the argument?

(A) removing from the herd and destroying any diseased animal as soon as it shows the typical symptoms of advanced BSE
(B) developing a drug that kills the agent that causes BSE, and then treating with that drug all cattle that might have the disease
(C) destroying all cattle in areas where BSE occurs and raising cattle only in areas to which BSE is known not to have spread
(D) developing a vaccine that confers lifelong immunity against BSE and giving it to all cattle, destroying in due course all those animals for which the vaccine protection came too late
(E) developing a diagnostic test that does identify any infected animal and destroying all animals found to be infected

10. Auto industry executive: Statistics show that cars that were built smaller after 1977 to make them more fuel-efficient had a higher incidence of accident-related fatalities than did their earlier, larger counterparts. For this reason we oppose recent guidelines that would require us to produce cars with higher fuel efficiency.

Which one of the following, if true, would constitute the strongest objection to the executive's argument?

(A) Even after 1977, large automobiles were frequently involved in accidents that caused death or serious injury.
(B) Although fatalities in accidents involving small cars have increased since 1977, the number of accidents has decreased.
(C) New computerized fuel systems can enable large cars to meet fuel efficiency standards established by the recent guidelines.
(D) Modern technology can make small cars more fuel-efficient today than at any other time in their production history.
(E) Fuel efficiency in models of large cars rose immediately after 1977 but has been declining ever since.

11. No one who lacks knowledge of a subject is competent to pass judgment on that subject. Since political know-how is a matter, not of adhering to technical rules, but of insight and style learned through apprenticeship and experience, only seasoned politicians are competent to judge whether a particular political policy is fair to all.

A major weakness of the argument is that it

(A) relies on a generalization about the characteristic that makes someone competent to pass judgment
(B) fails to give specific examples to illustrate how political know-how can be acquired
(C) uses the term "apprenticeship" to describe what is seldom a formalized relationship
(D) equates political know-how with understanding the social implications of political policies
(E) assumes that when inexperienced politicians set policy they are guided by the advice of more experienced politicians

12. Impact craters caused by meteorites smashing into Earth have been found all around the globe, but they have been found in the greatest density in geologically stable regions. This relatively greater abundance of securely identified craters in geologically stable regions must be explained by the lower rates of destructive geophysical processes in those regions.

The conclusion is properly drawn if which one of the following is assumed?

(A) A meteorite that strikes exactly the same spot as an earlier meteorite will obliterate all traces of the earlier impact.
(B) Rates of destructive geophysical processes within any given region vary markedly throughout geological time.
(C) The rate at which the Earth is struck by meteorites has greatly increased in geologically recent times.
(D) Actual meteorite impacts have been scattered fairly evenly over the Earth's surface in the course of Earth's geological history.
(E) The Earth's geologically stable regions have been studied more intensively by geologists than have its less stable regions.

GO ON TO THE NEXT PAGE.

13. That the policy of nuclear deterrence has worked thus far is unquestionable. Since the end of the Second World War, the very fact that there were nuclear armaments in existence has kept major powers from using nuclear weapons, for fear of starting a worldwide nuclear exchange that would make the land of the power initiating it uninhabitable. The proof is that a third world war between superpowers has not happened.

Which one of the following, if true, indicates a flaw in the argument?

(A) Maintaining a high level of nuclear armaments represents a significant drain on a country's economy.
(B) From what has happened in the past, it is impossible to infer with certainty what will happen in the future, so an accident could still trigger a third world war between superpowers.
(C) Continuing to produce nuclear weapons beyond the minimum needed for deterrence increases the likelihood of a nuclear accident.
(D) The major powers have engaged in many smaller-scale military operations since the end of the Second World War, while refraining from a nuclear confrontation.
(E) It cannot be known whether it was nuclear deterrence that worked, or some other factor, such as a recognition of the economic value of remaining at peace.

14. A survey of alumni of the class of 1960 at Aurora University yielded puzzling results. When asked to indicate their academic rank, half of the respondents reported that they were in the top quarter of the graduating class in 1960.

Which one of the following most helps account for the apparent contradiction above?

(A) A disproportionately large number of high-ranking alumni responded to the survey.
(B) Few, if any, respondents were mistaken about their class rank.
(C) Not all the alumni who were actually in the top quarter responded to the survey.
(D) Almost all of the alumni who graduated in 1960 responded to the survey.
(E) Academic rank at Aurora University was based on a number of considerations in addition to average grades.

15. M: It is almost impossible to find a person between the ages of 85 and 90 who primarily uses the left hand.

    Q: Seventy to ninety years ago, however, children were punished for using their left hands to eat or to write and were forced to use their right hands.

Q's response serves to counter any use by M of the evidence about 85 to 90 year olds in support of which one of the following hypotheses?

(A) Being born right-handed confers a survival advantage.
(B) Societal attitudes toward handedness differ at different times.
(C) Forcing a person to switch from a preferred hand is harmless.
(D) Handedness is a product of both genetic predisposition and social pressures.
(E) Physical habits learned in school often persist in old age.

16. The seventeenth-century physicist Sir Isaac Newton is remembered chiefly for his treatises on motion and gravity. But Newton also conducted experiments secretly for many years based on the arcane theories of alchemy, trying unsuccessfully to transmute common metals into gold and produce rejuvenating elixirs. If the alchemists of the seventeenth century had published the results of their experiments, chemistry in the eighteenth century would have been more advanced than it actually was.

Which one of the following assumptions would allow the conclusion concerning eighteenth-century chemistry to be properly drawn?

(A) Scientific progress is retarded by the reluctance of historians to acknowledge the failures of some of the great scientists.
(B) Advances in science are hastened when reports of experiments, whether successful or not, are available for review by other scientists.
(C) Newton's work on motion and gravity would not have gained wide acceptance if the results of his work in alchemy had also been made public.
(D) Increasing specialization within the sciences makes it difficult for scientists in one field to understand the principles of other fields.
(E) The seventeenth-century alchemists could have achieved their goals only if their experiments had been subjected to public scrutiny.

GO ON TO THE NEXT PAGE.

17. Sedimentary rock hardens within the earth's crust as layers of matter accumulate and the pressure of the layers above converts the layers below into rock. One particular layer of sedimentary rock that contains an unusual amount of the element iridium has been presented as support for a theory that a meteorite collided with the earth some sixty million years ago. Meteorites are rich in iridium compared to the earth's crust, and geologists theorize that a meteorite's collision with the earth raised a huge cloud of iridium-laden dust. The dust, they say, eventually settled to earth where it combined with other matter, and as new layers accumulated above it, it formed a layer of iridium-rich rock.

Which one of the following, if true, would counter the claim that the iridium-rich layer described in the passage is evidence for the meteorite collision theory?

(A) The huge dust cloud described in the passage would have blocked the transmission of sunlight and lowered the earth's temperature.
(B) A layer of sedimentary rock takes millions of years to harden.
(C) Layers of sedimentary rock are used to determine the dates of prehistoric events whether or not they contain iridium.
(D) Sixty million years ago there was a surge in volcanic activity in which the matter spewed from the volcanoes formed huge iridium-rich dust clouds.
(E) The iridium deposit occurred at about the same time that many animal species became extinct and some scientists have theorized that mass dinosaur extinctions were caused by a meteorite collision.

18. Mary, a veterinary student, has been assigned an experiment in mammalian physiology that would require her to take a healthy, anesthetized dog and subject it to a drastic blood loss in order to observe the physiological consequences of shock. The dog would neither regain consciousness nor survive the experiment. Mary decides not to do this assignment.

Mary's decision most closely accords with which one of the following principles?

(A) All other things being equal, gratuitously causing any animal to suffer pain is unjustified.
(B) Taking the life of an animal is not justifiable unless doing so would immediately assist in saving several animal lives or in protecting the health of a person.
(C) The only sufficient justification for experimenting on animals is that future animal suffering is thereby prevented.
(D) Practicing veterinarians have a professional obligation to strive to prevent the unnecessary death of an animal except in cases of severely ill or injured animals whose prospects for recovery are dim.
(E) No one is ever justified in acting with the sole intention of causing the death of a living thing, be it animal or human.

19. A tree's age can be determined by counting the annual growth rings in its trunk. Each ring represents one year, and the ring's thickness reveals the relative amount of rainfall that year. Archaeologists successfully used annual rings to determine the relative ages of ancient tombs at Pazyryk. Each tomb was constructed from freshly cut logs, and the tombs' builders were constrained by tradition to use only logs from trees growing in the sacred Pazyryk Valley.

Which one of the following, if true, contributes most to an explanation of the archaeologists' success in using annual rings to establish the relative ages of the tombs at the Pazyryk site?

(A) The Pazyryk tombs were all robbed during ancient times, but breakage of the tombs' seals allowed the seepage of water, which soon froze permanently, thereby preserving the tombs' remaining artifacts.
(B) The Pazyryk Valley, surrounded by extremely high mountains, has a distinctive yearly pattern of rainfall, and so trees growing in the Pazyryk Valley have annual rings that are quite distinct from trees growing in nearby valleys.
(C) Each log in the Pazyryk tombs has among its rings a distinctive sequence of twelve annual rings representing six drought years followed by three rainy years and three more drought years.
(D) The archaeologists determined that the youngest tree used in any of the tombs was 90 years old and that the oldest tree was 450 years old.
(E) All of the Pazyryk tombs contained cultural artifacts that can be dated to roughly 2300 years ago.

GO ON TO THE NEXT PAGE.

20. Experienced gardeners advise against planting snap peas after late April because peas do not develop properly in warm weather. This year, however, the weather was unusually cool into late June, and therefore the fact that these snap peas were planted in mid-May is unlikely to result in crop failure despite the experts' warnings.

The pattern of reasoning displayed above is most closely paralleled in which one of the following?

(A) According to many gardening authorities, tomatoes should not be planted near dill because doing so is likely to affect their taste adversely; however, since these tomatoes were grown near dill and taste fine, there is clearly no reason to pay much attention to the so-called experts' advice.

(B) Since African violets do not thrive in direct sunlight, it is said that in this region these plants should be placed in windows facing north rather than south; however, since these south-facing windows are well shaded by evergreen trees, the African violets placed in them are likely to grow satisfactorily.

(C) Where flowers are to be planted under shade trees, gardening experts often advise using impatiens since impatiens does well in conditions of shade; however, it is unlikely to do well under maple trees since maple tree roots are so near the surface that they absorb all available moisture.

(D) Most seeds tend to germinate at much higher rates when planted in warm soil than when planted in cold soil; spinach seeds, however, are unlikely to germinate properly if the soil is too warm, and therefore experts advise that spinach should be planted earlier than most vegetables.

(E) House plants generally grow best in pots slightly larger than their existing root systems, so the usual advice is to repot when roots first reach the sides of the pot; this rule should not be followed with amaryllis plants, however, because they are likely to do best with tightly compressed roots.

21. Whenever a major political scandal erupts before an election and voters blame the scandal on all parties about equally, virtually all incumbents, from whatever party, seeking reelection are returned to office. However, when voters blame such a scandal on only one party, incumbents from that party are likely to be defeated by challengers from other parties. The proportion of incumbents who seek reelection is high and remarkably constant from election to election.

If the voters' reactions are guided by a principle, which one of the following principles would best account for the contrast in reactions described above?

(A) Whenever one incumbent is responsible for one major political scandal and another incumbent is responsible for another, the consequences for the two incumbents should be the same.

(B) When a major political scandal is blamed on incumbents from all parties, that judgment is more accurate than any judgment that incumbents from only one party are to blame.

(C) Incumbents who are rightly blamed for a major political scandal should not seek reelection, but if they do, they should not be returned to office.

(D) Major political scandals can practically always be blamed on incumbents, but whether those incumbents should be voted out of office depends on who their challengers are.

(E) When major political scandals are less the responsibility of individual incumbents than of the parties to which they belong, whatever party was responsible must be penalized when possible.

GO ON TO THE NEXT PAGE.

22. Once people habitually engaged in conversation; now the television competes for their attention. When the television is on, communication between family members stops. Where there is no communication, family ties become frayed and eventually snap. Therefore, the only solution is to get rid of the television.

Which one of the following is most closely parallel in its reasoning to the flawed reasoning in the argument above?

(A) Once friendships thrived on shared leisure time. But contemporary economic pressures minimize the amount of free time people have and thus jeopardize many friendships.

(B) Once people listened to the radio while pursuing other activities. Now they passively watch television. Therefore, radio was less distracting for most people than television is.

(C) Once sports enthusiasts regularly engaged in sports, but now they watch spectator sports when they could be getting physical exercise. Without physical exercise, health deteriorates. Therefore, the only remedy is to eliminate spectator sports.

(D) Once people were willing to tailor their day to the constraints of a bus or train schedule; now they are spoiled by the private car. The only solution is for government to offer financial incentives to encourage the use of public transportation.

(E) Once people did their shopping in urban retail districts, where they combined their shopping with other errands. Now many people shop in suburban malls, where they concentrate on shopping exclusively. Therefore, shopping has become a leisure time activity.

23. In essence, all rent-control policies involve specifying a maximum rent that a landlord may charge for a dwelling. The rationale for controlling rents is to protect tenants in situations where limited supply will cause rents to rise sharply in the face of increased demand. However, although rent control may help some tenants in the short run, it affects the rental-housing market adversely in the long run because landlords become reluctant to maintain the quality of their existing properties and even more reluctant to have additional rental-housing units built.

Which one of the following, if true, best explains the landlords' reluctance described above?

(A) Tenants prefer low-quality accommodations with rent control to high-quality accommodations without it.

(B) Rent control makes it very difficult for landlords to achieve reasonable returns on any investments in maintenance or in new construction.

(C) Rent control is a common practice even though it does nothing to alleviate shortages in rental housing.

(D) Rent control is generally introduced for political reasons and it takes political action to have it lifted again.

(E) Tenants prefer rent control to the alternative of receiving direct government subsidies toward rents they cannot afford.

GO ON TO THE NEXT PAGE.

24. Certain minor peculiarities of language are used unconsciously by poets. If such peculiarities appear in the works of more than one poet, they are likely to reflect the language in common use during the poets' time. However, if they appear in the work of only one poet, they are likely to be personal idiosyncrasies. As such, they can provide a kind of "fingerprint" that allows scholars, by comparing a poem of previously unknown authorship to the work of a particular known poet, to identify the poem as the work of that poet.

For which one of the following reasons can the test described above never provide conclusive proof of the authorship of any poem?

(A) The labor of analyzing peculiarities of language both in the work of a known poet and in a poem of unknown authorship would not be undertaken unless other evidence already suggested that the poem of unknown authorship was written by the known poet.

(B) A peculiarity of language that might be used as an identifying mark is likely to be widely scattered in the work of a poet, so that a single poem not known to have been written by that poet might not include that peculiarity.

(C) A peculiarity of language in a poem of unknown authorship could be evidence either that the poem was written by the one author known to use that peculiarity or that the peculiarity was not unique to that author.

(D) Minor peculiarities of language contribute far less to the literary effect of any poem than such factors as poetic form, subject matter, and deliberately chosen wording.

(E) A poet's use of some peculiarities of language might have been unconscious in some poems and conscious in other poems, and the two uses would be indistinguishable to scholars at a later date.

25. Because of the recent transformation of the market, Quore, Inc., must increase productivity 10 percent over the course of the next two years, or it will certainly go bankrupt. In fact, however, Quore's production structure is such that if a 10 percent productivity increase is possible, then a 20 percent increase is attainable.

If the statements above are true, which one of the following must on the basis of them also be true?

(A) It is only Quore's production structure that makes it possible for Quore to survive the transformation of the market.

(B) Quore will not go bankrupt if it achieves a productivity increase of 20 percent over the next two years.

(C) If the market had not been transformed, Quore would have required no productivity increase in order to avoid bankruptcy.

(D) Because of the transformation of the market, Quore will achieve a productivity increase of 10 percent over the next two years.

(E) If a 20 percent productivity increase is unattainable for Quore, then it must go bankrupt.

S T O P

IF YOU FINISH BEFORE TIME IS CALLED, YOU MAY CHECK YOUR WORK ON THIS SECTION ONLY.
DO NOT WORK ON ANY OTHER SECTION IN THE TEST.

SECTION II
Time—35 minutes
24 Questions

Directions: Each group of questions in this section is based on a set of conditions. In answering some of the questions, it may be useful to draw a rough diagram. Choose the response that most accurately and completely answers each question and blacken the corresponding space on your answer sheet.

Questions 1–6

John receives one grade for each of the following six courses: economics, geology, history, Italian, physics, and Russian. From highest to lowest, the possible grades are A, B, C, D, and E. E is the only failing grade. Two letter grades are consecutive if and only if they are adjacent in the alphabet.
    John's grades in geology and physics are consecutive. His grades in Italian and Russian are consecutive.
    He receives a higher grade in economics than in history.
    He receives a higher grade in geology than in physics.

1. If John receives the same grade in economics and Italian, and if he fails Russian, which one of the following must be true?

  (A) John's geology grade is a B.
  (B) John's history grade is a D.
  (C) John's history grade is an E.
  (D) John's physics grade is a B.
  (E) John's physics grade is a C.

2. If John passes all his courses and receives a higher grade in geology than in either language, which one of the following must be true?

  (A) He receives exactly one A.
  (B) He receives exactly one B.
  (C) He receives exactly two Bs.
  (D) He receives at least one B and at least one C.
  (E) He receives at least one C and at least one D.

3. If John receives a higher grade in physics than in economics and receives a higher grade in economics than in either language, which one of the following allows all six of his grades to be determined?

  (A) His grade in history is D.
  (B) His grade in Italian is D.
  (C) His grades in history and Italian are identical.
  (D) His grades in history and Russian are identical.
  (E) His grade in history is higher than his grade in Russian.

4. If John receives a higher grade in physics than in economics and receives a higher grade in history than in Italian, exactly how many of his grades can be determined?

  (A) 2
  (B) 3
  (C) 4
  (D) 5
  (E) 6

5. Assume that John's grade in physics is higher than his grade in Italian and consecutive with it and that his grades in Russian and physics differ. Which one of the following must be true?

  (A) John receives both an A and a B.
  (B) John receives both an A and a C.
  (C) John receives both a B and a D.
  (D) John receives both a B and an E.
  (E) John receives both a D and an E.

6. Assume that John receives a lower grade in economics than in physics. He must have failed at least one course if which one of the following is also true?

  (A) He receives a lower grade in Italian than in economics.
  (B) He receives a lower grade in Italian than in physics.
  (C) He receives a lower grade in physics than in Italian.
  (D) He receives a lower grade in Russian than in economics.
  (E) He receives a lower grade in Russian than in history.

GO ON TO THE NEXT PAGE.

Questions 7–11

A store sells shirts only in small, medium, and large sizes, and only in red, yellow, and blue colors. Casey buys exactly three shirts from the store.
　　A shirt type consists of both a size and a color.
　　Casey does not buy two shirts of the same type.
　　Casey does not buy both a small shirt and a large shirt.
　　No small red shirts are available.
　　No large blue shirts are available.

7. Which one of the following must be false?

　(A)　Two of the shirts that Casey buys are small and two are red.
　(B)　Two of the shirts that Casey buys are medium and two are red.
　(C)　Two of the shirts that Casey buys are large and two are red.
　(D)　Two of the shirts that Casey buys are small, one is yellow, and one is blue.
　(E)　Two of the shirts that Casey buys are medium, one is yellow, and one is blue.

8. If Casey buys a small blue shirt, which one of the following must be false?

　(A)　Casey buys two blue shirts.
　(B)　Casey buys two red shirts.
　(C)　Casey buys two yellow shirts.
　(D)　Casey buys two small shirts.
　(E)　Casey buys two medium shirts.

9. If Casey does not buy a medium yellow shirt, which one of the following must be true?

　(A)　Casey buys either a medium red shirt or a small blue shirt.
　(B)　Casey buys either a medium red shirt or a medium blue shirt.
　(C)　Casey buys either a large red shirt or a small blue shirt.
　(D)　Casey buys either a large red shirt or a medium red shirt.
　(E)　Casey buys either a large yellow shirt or a small yellow shirt.

10. If Casey buys exactly one medium shirt and does not buy two shirts of the same color, then she cannot buy which one of the following?

　(A)　a medium red shirt
　(B)　a medium yellow shirt
　(C)　a medium blue shirt
　(D)　a large red shirt
　(E)　a large yellow shirt

11. If neither large red shirts nor small blue shirts are available, which one of the following must Casey buy?

　(A)　a red shirt
　(B)　a medium yellow shirt
　(C)　either a large shirt or a small shirt
　(D)　either a medium red shirt or a medium blue shirt
　(E)　either a large yellow shirt or a medium blue shirt

GO ON TO THE NEXT PAGE.

Questions 12–17

A hobbyist is stocking her aquarium with exactly three fish of different types and with exactly two species of plants. The only fish under consideration are a G, an H, a J, a K, and an L, and the only kinds of plants under consideration are of the species W, X, Y, and Z. She will observe the following conditions:

If she selects the G, she can select neither the H nor a Y.
She cannot select the H unless she selects the K.
She cannot select the J unless she selects a W.
If she selects the K, she must select an X.

12. Which one of the following is an acceptable selection of fish and plants for the aquarium?

	Fish	Plants
(A)	G, H, K	W, Y
(B)	G, J, K	W, X
(C)	G, J, L	X, Z
(D)	H, J, L	W, Z
(E)	H, K, L	Y, Z

13. If the hobbyist selects the H, which one of the following must also be true?

(A) She selects at least one W.
(B) She selects at least one X.
(C) She selects the J, but no Y's.
(D) She selects the K, but no X's.
(E) She selects at least one X, but no Y's.

14. If the hobbyist selects both X's and Z's, which one of the following could be the group of fish she selects?

(A) G, H, K
(B) G, J, K
(C) G, K, L
(D) H, J, L
(E) J, K, L

15. The hobbyist could select any of the following groups of fish for the aquarium EXCEPT

(A) G, K, L
(B) H, J, K
(C) H, J, L
(D) H, K, L
(E) J, K, L

16. If the hobbyist selects a Y, which one of the following must be the group of fish she selects?

(A) G, H, K
(B) H, J, K
(C) H, J, L
(D) H, K, L
(E) J, K, L

17. The hobbyist could select any of the following plant combinations EXCEPT

(A) W and X
(B) W and Y
(C) W and Z
(D) X and Y
(E) X and Z

GO ON TO THE NEXT PAGE.

Questions 18–24

A committee ranks five towns—Palmdale, Quietville, Riverdale, Seaside, Tidetown—from first (best) to fifth (worst) on each of three criteria: climate, location, friendliness.

For each of the three criteria, none of the five towns receives the same ranking as any other town does.

In climate, Tidetown is ranked third, and Seaside fourth.

In location, Quietville is ranked second, Riverdale third, Palmdale fourth.

In friendliness, Tidetown's ranking is better than Palmdale's, Quietville is ranked fourth, and Seaside fifth.

Riverdale receives a better ranking in climate than in friendliness.

Quietville's three rankings are all different from each other.

18. Which one of the following is a complete and accurate list of the rankings any one of which could be the ranking on climate given to Riverdale?

(A) first
(B) first, second
(C) first, fifth
(D) second, fifth
(E) first, second, fifth

19. Which one of the following is a town that CANNOT be ranked fifth on any one of the three criteria?

(A) Palmdale
(B) Quietville
(C) Riverdale
(D) Seaside
(E) Tidetown

20. Which one of the following could be true?

(A) Palmdale is ranked first in both climate and friendliness.
(B) Quietville is ranked second in both climate and location.
(C) Riverdale is ranked first in climate and third in both location and friendliness.
(D) Seaside is ranked fifth in friendliness and fourth in both climate and location.
(E) Tidetown is ranked third in both climate and friendliness.

21. If Quietville is ranked first in climate, then it must be true that

(A) Palmdale is ranked second in climate
(B) Palmdale is ranked third in friendliness
(C) Riverdale is ranked second in friendliness
(D) Riverdale is ranked third in friendliness
(E) Tidetown is ranked fifth in location

22. If Palmdale is ranked second in climate, then which one of the following can be true?

(A) Palmdale is ranked second in friendliness.
(B) Quietville is ranked first in climate.
(C) Riverdale is ranked first in friendliness.
(D) Riverdale is ranked fifth in climate.
(E) Tidetown is ranked third in friendliness.

23. If Tidetown is ranked first in location and Riverdale is ranked second in friendliness, then it is possible to deduce with certainty all three rankings for exactly how many of the towns?

(A) One
(B) Two
(C) Three
(D) Four
(E) Five

24. Which one of the following statements CANNOT be true?

(A) Palmdale is ranked first in climate.
(B) Quietville is ranked fifth in climate.
(C) Riverdale is ranked third in friendliness.
(D) Seaside is ranked first in location.
(E) Tidetown is ranked second in friendliness.

S T O P

IF YOU FINISH BEFORE TIME IS CALLED, YOU MAY CHECK YOUR WORK ON THIS SECTION ONLY.
DO NOT WORK ON ANY OTHER SECTION IN THE TEST.

SECTION III
Time—35 minutes
25 Questions

Directions: The questions in this section are based on the reasoning contained in brief statements or passages. For some questions, more than one of the choices could conceivably answer the question. However, you are to choose the best answer; that is, the response that most accurately and completely answers the question. You should not make assumptions that are by commonsense standards implausible, superfluous, or incompatible with the passage. After you have chosen the best answer, blacken the corresponding space on your answer sheet.

1. Terry: If you want to get a decent job, you should go to college.

   Mark: That is not true. There are other reasons to go to college than wanting to get a good job.

   Mark's response shows that he interpreted Terry's remarks to mean that

   (A) college is one of many places to get trained for a job
   (B) decent jobs are obtained only by persons who have gone to college
   (C) wanting to get a decent job is the only reason for going to college
   (D) training for decent jobs is available only at colleges
   (E) all people who want decent jobs go to college

2. Several studies have shown that hospitals are not all equally successful: patients are much more likely to die in some of them than in others. Since the hospitals in the studies had approximately equal per-patient funding, differences in the quality of care provided by hospital staff are probably responsible for the differences in mortality rates.

   Which one of the following, if true, casts the most doubt on the conclusion drawn above?

   (A) The staff in some of the hospitals studied had earned more advanced degrees, on average, than the staff in the other hospitals.
   (B) Patient populations vary substantially in average severity of illness from hospital to hospital.
   (C) The average number of years that staff members stay on at a given job varies considerably from one hospital to another.
   (D) Approximately the same surgical procedures were performed in each of the hospitals covered in the studies.
   (E) Mortality rates for hospital patients do not vary considerably from one region of the country to another.

Questions 3–4

The United States government generally tries to protect valuable natural resources. But one resource has been ignored for too long. In the United States, each bushel of corn produced might result in the loss of as much as two bushels of topsoil. Moreover, in the last 100 years, the topsoil in many states, which once was about fourteen inches thick, has been eroded to only six or eight inches. Nonetheless, federal expenditures for nationwide soil conservation programs have remained at ridiculously low levels. Total federal expenditures for nationwide soil conservation programs have been less than the allocations of some individual states.

3. Which one of the following best expresses the main point of the argument?

   (A) Corn is not a cost-effective product and substitutes should be found where possible.
   (B) A layer of topsoil only six to eight inches thick cannot support the continued cultivation of corn.
   (C) Soil conservation is a responsibility of the federal government, not the states.
   (D) The federal government's expenditures for soil conservation in the various states have been inequitable.
   (E) The federal government should spend much more on soil conservation than it has been spending.

4. In stating the argument, the author does which one of the following?

   (A) makes a detailed statistical projection of future topsoil loss
   (B) makes a generalization about total reduction in topsoil depth in all states
   (C) assumes that the United States government does not place a high value on its natural resources
   (D) refrains from using slanted language concerning the level of federal expenditures
   (E) compares state expenditures with federal expenditures

GO ON TO THE NEXT PAGE.

5. Animals with a certain behavioral disorder have unusually high levels of aluminum in their brain tissue. Since a silicon-based compound binds to aluminum and prevents it from affecting the brain tissue, animals can be cured of the disorder by being treated with the compound.

The argument is based on which one of the following assumptions?

(A) Animals with the disorder have unusually high but invariable levels of aluminum in their brain tissue.
(B) Aluminum is the cause of the disorder rather than merely an effect of it.
(C) Introducing the compound into the brain tissue has no side effects.
(D) The amount of the compound needed to neutralize the aluminum in an animal's brain tissue varies depending upon the species.
(E) Aluminum is never present in normal brain tissue.

6. As air-breathing mammals, whales must once have lived on land and needed hind limbs capable of supporting the mammals' weight. Whales have the bare remnants of a pelvis. If animals have a pelvis, we expect them to have hind limbs. A newly discovered fossilized whale skeleton has very fragile hind limbs that could not have supported the animal's weight on land. This skeleton had a partial pelvis.

If the statements above are true, which one of the following, if also true, would most strongly support the conclusion that the fragile hind limbs are remnants of limbs that land-dwelling whales once had?

(A) Whale bones older than the fossilized hind limbs confirm that ancient whales had full pelvises.
(B) No skeletons of ancient whales with intact hind limbs capable of supporting the mammals' weight have ever been found.
(C) Scientists are uncertain whether the apparently nonfunctioning limbs of other early mammals derived from once-functioning limbs of their ancestors.
(D) Other large-bodied mammals like seals and sea lions maneuver on beaches and rocky coasts without fully functioning hind limbs.
(E) Some smaller sea-dwelling mammals, such as modern dolphins, have no visible indications of hind limbs.

7. The stated goal of the government's funding program for the arts is to encourage the creation of works of artistic excellence. Senator Beton claims, however, that a government-funded artwork can never reflect the independent artistic conscience of the artist because artists, like anyone else who accepts financial support, will inevitably try to please those who control the distribution of that support. Senator Beton concludes that government funding of the arts not only is a burden on taxpayers but also cannot lead to the creation of works of true artistic excellence.

Which one of the following is an assumption on which Senator Beton's argument is based?

(A) Most taxpayers have little or no interest in the creation of works of true artistic excellence.
(B) Government funding of the arts is more generous than other financial support most artists receive.
(C) Distribution of government funds for the arts is based on a broad agreement as to what constitutes artistic excellence.
(D) Once an artist has produced works of true artistic excellence, he or she will never accept government funding.
(E) A contemporary work of art that does not reflect the independent artistic conscience of the artist cannot be a work of true artistic excellence.

GO ON TO THE NEXT PAGE.

8. Older United States automobiles have been identified as contributing disproportionately to global air pollution. The requirement in many jurisdictions that automobiles pass emission-control inspections has had the effect of taking many such automobiles out of service in the United States, as they fail inspection and their owners opt to buy newer automobiles. Thus the burden of pollution such older United States automobiles contribute to the global atmosphere will be gradually reduced over the next decade.

Which one of the following, if true, most seriously weakens the argument?

(A) It is impossible to separate the air of one country or jurisdiction from that of others, since air currents circle the globe.

(B) When automobiles that are now new become older, they will, because of a design change, cause less air pollution than older automobiles do now.

(C) There is a thriving market for used older United States automobiles that are exported to regions that have no emission-control regulations.

(D) The number of jurisdictions in the United States requiring automobiles to pass emission-control inspections is no longer increasing.

(E) Even if all the older automobiles in the United States were retired from service, air pollution from United States automobiles could still increase if the total number of automobiles in use should increase significantly.

9. The journalistic practice of fabricating remarks after an interview and printing them within quotation marks, as if they were the interviewee's own words, has been decried as a form of unfair misrepresentation. However, people's actual spoken remarks rarely convey their ideas as clearly as does a distillation of those ideas crafted, after an interview, by a skilled writer. Therefore, since this practice avoids the more serious misrepresentation that would occur if people's exact words were quoted but their ideas only partially expressed, it is entirely defensible.

Which one of the following is a questionable technique used in the argument?

(A) answering an exaggerated charge by undermining the personal authority of those who made that charge

(B) claiming that the prestige of a profession provides ample grounds for dismissing criticisms of that profession

(C) offering as an adequate defense of a practice an observation that discredits only one of several possible alternatives to that practice

(D) concluding that a practice is right on the grounds that it is necessary

(E) using the opponent's admission that a practice is sometimes appropriate as conclusive proof that that practice is never inappropriate

10. The reforms to improve the quality of public education that have been initiated on the part of suppliers of public education have been insufficient. Therefore, reforms must be demanded by consumers. Parents should be given government vouchers with which to pay for their children's education and should be allowed to choose the schools at which the vouchers will be spent. To attract students, academically underachieving schools will be forced to improve their academic offerings.

The argument assumes that

(A) in selecting schools parents would tend to prefer a reasonable level of academic quality to greater sports opportunities or more convenient location

(B) improvement in the academic offerings of schools will be enforced by the discipline of the job market in which graduating students compete

(C) there is a single best way to educate students

(D) children are able to recognize which schools are better and would influence their parents' decisions

(E) schools would each improve all of their academic offerings and would not tend to specialize in one particular field to the exclusion of others

GO ON TO THE NEXT PAGE.

11. Professor Smith published a paper arguing that a chemical found in minute quantities in most drinking water had an adverse effect on the human nervous system. Existing scientific theory held that no such effect was possible because there was no neural mechanism for bringing it about. Several papers by well-known scientists in the field followed, unanimously purporting to prove Professor Smith wrong. This clearly shows that the scientific establishment was threatened by Professor Smith's work and conspired to discredit it.

Which one of the following is the central flaw in the argument given by the author of the passage?

(A) The author passes over the possibility that Professor Smith had much to gain should Professor Smith's discovery have found general acceptance.

(B) The author fails to mention whether or not Professor Smith knew that the existence of the alleged new effect was incompatible with established scientific theory.

(C) The author fails to show why the other scientists could not have been presenting evidence in order to establish the truth of the matter.

(D) The author neglects to clarify what his or her relationship to Professor Smith is.

(E) The author fails to indicate what, if any, effect the publication of Professor Smith's paper had on the public's confidence in the safety of most drinking water.

12. The number of North American children who are obese—that is, who have more body fat than do 85 percent of North American children their age—is steadily increasing, according to four major studies conducted over the past 15 years.

If the finding reported above is correct, it can be properly concluded that

(A) when four major studies all produce similar results, those studies must be accurate

(B) North American children have been progressively less physically active over the past 15 years

(C) the number of North American children who are not obese increased over the past 15 years

(D) over the past 15 years, the number of North American children who are underweight has declined

(E) the incidence of obesity in North American children tends to increase as the children grow older

13. Economist: Money, no matter what its form and in almost every culture in which it has been used, derives its value from its scarcity, whether real or perceived.

Anthropologist: But cowrie shells formed the major currency in the Solomon Island economy of the Kwara'ae, and unlimited numbers of these shells washed up daily on the beaches to which the Kwara'ae had access.

Which one of the following, if true about the Kwara'ae, best serves to resolve the apparently conflicting positions cited above?

(A) During festivals they exchanged strings of cowrie-shell money with each other as part of a traditional ritual that honored their elders.

(B) They considered porpoise teeth valuable, and these were generally threaded on strings to be worn as jewelry.

(C) The shells used as money by men were not always from the same species of cowrie as those used as money by women.

(D) They accepted as money only cowrie shells that were polished and carved by a neighboring people, and such shell preparation required both time and skilled labor.

(E) After Western traders brought money in the form of precious-metal coins to the Solomon Islands, cowrie-shell money continued to be used as one of the major media of exchange for both goods and services.

14. School superintendent: It is a sad fact that, until now, entry into the academically best high school in our district has been restricted to the children of people who were wealthy enough to pay the high tuition. Parents who were previously denied the option of sending their children to this school now have this option, since I am replacing the tuition requirement with a requirement that allows only those who live in the neighborhood of the school to attend.

The superintendent's claim about the effect of replacing the tuition requirement relies on the assumption that

(A) the residents of the school's neighborhood tend to be wealthy

(B) people other than those wealthy enough to have paid the old tuition are able to live in the neighborhood of the school

(C) people less wealthy than those who were able to pay the old tuition are in the majority in the district

(D) there are no high schools in the district other than the one referred to by the superintendent

(E) there are many people not wealthy enough to have paid the old tuition who wish to have their children attend the school

GO ON TO THE NEXT PAGE.

15. The Scorpio Miser with its special high-efficiency engine costs more to buy than the standard Scorpio sports car. At current fuel prices, a buyer choosing the Miser would have to drive it 60,000 miles to make up the difference in purchase price through savings on fuel. It follows that, if fuel prices fell, it would take fewer miles to reach the break-even point.

Which one of the following arguments contains an error of reasoning similar to that in the argument above?

(A) The true annual rate of earnings on an interest-bearing account is the annual rate of interest less the annual rate of inflation. Consequently, if the rate of inflation drops, the rate of interest can be reduced by an equal amount without there being a change in the true rate of earnings.

(B) For retail food stores, the Polar freezer, unlike the Arctic freezer, provides a consistent temperature that allows the store to carry premium frozen foods. Though the Polar freezer uses more electricity, there is a bigger profit on premium foods. Thus, if electricity rates fell, a lower volume of premium-food sales could justify choosing the Polar freezer.

(C) With the Roadmaker, a crew can repave a mile of decayed road in less time than with the competing model, which is, however, much less expensive. Reduced staffing levels made possible by the Roadmaker eventually compensate for its higher price. Therefore, the Roadmaker is especially advantageous where average wages are low.

(D) The improved strain of the Northland apple tree bears fruit younger and lives longer than the standard strain. The standard strain does grow larger at maturity, but to allow for this, standard trees must be spaced farther apart. Therefore, new plantings should all be of the improved strain.

(E) Stocks pay dividends, which vary from year to year depending on profits made. Bonds pay interest, which remains constant from year to year. Therefore, since the interest earned on bonds does not decrease when economic conditions decline, investors interested in a reliable income should choose bonds.

16. Approximately 7.6 million women who earn incomes have preschool-age children, and approximately 6.4 million women are the sole income earners for their families. These figures indicate that there are comparatively few income-earning women who have preschool-age children but are not the sole income earners for their families.

A major flaw in the reasoning is that it

(A) relies on figures that are too imprecise to support the conclusion drawn

(B) overlooks the possibility that there is little or no overlap between the two populations of women cited

(C) fails to indicate whether the difference between the two figures cited will tend to remain stable over time

(D) ignores the possibility that families with preschool-age children might also have older children

(E) provides no information on families in which men are the sole income earners

17. Being articulate has been equated with having a large vocabulary. Actually, however, people with large vocabularies have no incentive for, and tend not to engage in, the kind of creative linguistic self-expression that is required when no available words seem adequate. Thus a large vocabulary is a hindrance to using language in a truly articulate way.

Which one of the following is an assumption made in the argument?

(A) When people are truly articulate, they have the capacity to express themselves in situations in which their vocabularies seem inadequate.

(B) People who are able to express themselves creatively in new situations have little incentive to acquire large vocabularies.

(C) The most articulate people are people who have large vocabularies but also are able to express themselves creatively when the situation demands it.

(D) In educating people to be more articulate, it would be futile to try to increase the size of their vocabularies.

(E) In unfamiliar situations, even people with large vocabularies often do not have specifically suitable words available.

GO ON TO THE NEXT PAGE.

Questions 18–19

Dr. Schilling: Those who advocate replacing my country's private health insurance system with nationalized health insurance because of the rising costs of medical care fail to consider the high human costs that consumers pay in countries with nationalized insurance: access to high-technology medicine is restricted. Kidney transplants and open-heart surgery—familiar life-saving procedures—are rationed. People are denied their right to treatments they want and need.

Dr. Laforte: Your country's reliance on private health insurance denies access even to basic, conventional medicine to the many people who cannot afford adequate health coverage. With nationalized insurance, rich and poor have equal access to life-saving medical procedures, and people's right to decent medical treatment regardless of income is not violated.

18.   Dr. Schilling's and Dr. Laforte's statements provide the most support for holding that they would disagree about the truth of which one of the following?

(A)   People's rights are violated less when they are denied an available medical treatment they need because they lack the means to pay for it than when they are denied such treatment on noneconomic grounds.

(B)   Where health insurance is provided by private insurance companies, people who are wealthy generally receive better health care than do people who are unable to afford health insurance.

(C)   In countries that rely primarily on private health insurance to pay for medical costs, most people who would benefit from a kidney transplant receive one.

(D)   In countries with nationalized health insurance, no one who needs a familiar medical treatment in order to stay alive is denied that treatment.

(E)   Anyone who wants a particular medical treatment has a right to receive that treatment.

19.   In responding to Dr. Schilling, Dr. Laforte employs which one of the following argumentative strategies?

(A)   showing that the objections raised by Dr. Schilling have no bearing on the question of which of the two systems under consideration is the superior system

(B)   calling into question Dr. Schilling's status as an authority on the issue of whether consumers' access to medical treatments is restricted in countries with nationalized health insurance

(C)   producing counterexamples to Dr. Schilling's claims that nationalized health insurance schemes extract high human costs from consumers

(D)   demonstrating that Dr. Schilling's reasoning is persuasive only because of his ambiguous use of the key word "consumer"

(E)   showing that the force of Dr. Schilling's criticism depends on construing the key notion of access in a particular limited way

GO ON TO THE NEXT PAGE.

20. A certain viral infection is widespread among children, and about 30 percent of children infected with the virus develop middle ear infections. Antibiotics, although effective in treating bacterial infections, have no effect on the virus. Yet when middle ear infections in children infected with the virus are treated with antibiotics, the ear infections often clear up.

Which one of the following most helps to explain the success of the treatments with antibiotics?

(A) Although some types of antibiotics fail to clear up certain infections, other types of antibiotics might provide effective treatment for those infections.
(B) Children infected with the virus are particularly susceptible to bacteria that infect the middle ear.
(C) Many children who develop middle ear infections are not infected with the virus.
(D) Most viral infections are more difficult to treat than are most bacterial infections.
(E) Among children not infected with the virus, fewer than 30 percent develop middle ear infections.

21. Naturalist: For decades we have known that the tuatara, a New Zealand reptile, have been approaching extinction on the South Island. But since South Island tuatara were thought to be of the same species as North Island tuatara there was no need to protect them. But new research indicates that the South Island tuatara are a distinct species, found only in that location. Because it is now known that if the South Island tuatara are lost an entire species will thereby be lost, human beings are now obliged to prevent their extinction, even if it means killing many of their unendangered natural predators.

Which one of the following principles most helps to justify the naturalists' argumentation?

(A) In order to maximize the number of living things on Earth, steps should be taken to preserve all local populations of animals.
(B) When an animal is in danger of dying, there is an obligation to help save its life, if doing so would not interfere with the health or well-being of other animals or people.
(C) The threat of local extinction imposes no obligation to try to prevent that extinction, whereas the threat of global extinction does impose such an obligation.
(D) Human activities that either intentionally or unintentionally threaten the survival of an animal species ought to be curtailed.
(E) Species that are found in only one circumscribed geographical region ought to be given more care and attention than are other species because they are more vulnerable to extinction.

22. Nursing schools cannot attract a greater number of able applicants than they currently do unless the problems of low wages and high-stress working conditions in the nursing profession are solved. If the pool of able applicants to nursing school does not increase beyond the current level, either the profession will have to lower its entrance standards, or there will soon be an acute shortage of nurses. It is not certain, however, that lowering entrance standards will avert a shortage. It is clear that with either a shortage of nurses or lowered entrance standards for the profession, the current high quality of health care cannot be maintained.

Which one of the following can be properly inferred from the passage?

(A) If the nursing profession solves the problems of low wages and high-stress working conditions, it will attract able applicants in greater numbers than it currently does.
(B) The nursing profession will have to lower its entrance standards if the pool of able applicants to nursing school does not increase beyond the current level.
(C) If the nursing profession solves the problems of low wages and high-stress working conditions, high quality health care will be maintained.
(D) If the nursing profession fails to solve the problems of low wages and high-stress working conditions, there will soon be an acute shortage of nurses.
(E) The current high quality of health care will not be maintained if the problems of low wages and high-stress working conditions in the nursing profession are not solved.

GO ON TO THE NEXT PAGE.

Questions 23–24

There are about 75 brands of microwave popcorn on the market; altogether, they account for a little over half of the money from sales of microwave food products. It takes three minutes to pop corn in the microwave, compared to seven minutes to pop corn conventionally. Yet by weight, microwave popcorn typically costs over five times as much as conventional popcorn. Judging by the popularity of microwave popcorn, many people are willing to pay a high price for just a little additional convenience.

23. If the statements in the passage are true, which one of the following must also be true?

(A) No single brand of microwave popcorn accounts for a large share of microwave food product sales.

(B) There are more brands of microwave popcorn on the market than there are of any other microwave food product.

(C) By volume, more microwave popcorn is sold than is conventional popcorn.

(D) More money is spent on microwave food products that take three minutes or less to cook than on microwave food products that take longer to cook.

(E) Of the total number of microwave food products on the market, most are microwave popcorn products.

24. Which one of the following statements, if true, would call into question the conclusion in the passage?

(A) More than 50 percent of popcorn purchasers buy conventional popcorn rather than microwave popcorn.

(B) Most people who prefer microwave popcorn do so because it is less fattening than popcorn that is popped conventionally in oil.

(C) The price of microwave popcorn reflects its packaging more than it reflects the quality of the popcorn contained in the package.

(D) The ratio of unpopped kernels to popped kernels is generally the same whether popcorn is popped in a microwave or conventionally in oil.

(E) Because microwave popcorn contains additives not contained in conventional popcorn, microwave popcorn weighs more than an equal volume of conventional popcorn.

25. Situation: In the island nation of Bezun, the government taxes gasoline heavily in order to induce people not to drive. It uses the revenue from the gasoline tax to subsidize electricity in order to reduce prices charged for electricity.

Analysis: The greater the success achieved in meeting the first of these objectives, the less will be the success achieved in meeting the second.

The analysis provided for the situation above would be most appropriate in which one of the following situations?

(A) A library charges a late fee in order to induce borrowers to return books promptly. The library uses revenue from the late fee to send reminders to tardy borrowers in order to reduce the incidence of overdue books.

(B) A mail-order store imposes a stiff surcharge for overnight delivery in order to limit use of this option. The store uses revenue from the surcharge to pay the extra expenses it incurs for providing the overnight delivery service.

(C) The park management charges an admission fee so that a park's users will contribute to the park's upkeep. In order to keep admission fees low, the management does not finance any new projects from them.

(D) A restaurant adds a service charge in order to spare customers the trouble of individual tips. The service charge is then shared among the restaurant's workers in order to augment their low hourly wages.

(E) The highway administration charges a toll for crossing a bridge in order to get motorists to use other routes. It uses the revenue from that toll to generate a reserve fund in order to be able one day to build a new bridge.

S T O P

**IF YOU FINISH BEFORE TIME IS CALLED, YOU MAY CHECK YOUR WORK ON THIS SECTION ONLY.
DO NOT WORK ON ANY OTHER SECTION IN THE TEST.**

SECTION IV

Time—35 minutes

27 Questions

Directions: Each passage in this section is followed by a group of questions to be answered on the basis of what is stated or implied in the passage. For some of the questions, more than one of the choices could conceivably answer the question. However, you are to choose the best answer; that is, the response that most accurately and completely answers the question, and blacken the corresponding space on your answer sheet.

Governments of developing countries occasionally enter into economic development agreements with foreign investors who provide capital and technological expertise that may not be
(5) readily available in such countries. Besides the normal economic risk that accompanies such enterprises, investors face the additional risk that the host government may attempt unilaterally to change in its favor the terms of the agreement or
(10) even to terminate the agreement altogether and appropriate the project for itself. In order to make economic development agreements more attractive to investors, some developing countries have attempted to strengthen the security of such
(15) agreements with clauses specifying that the agreements will be governed by "general principles of law recognized by civilized nations"—a set of legal principles or rules shared by the world's major legal systems. However, advocates of governments'
(20) freedom to modify or terminate such agreements argue that these agreements fall within a special class of contracts known as administrative contracts, a concept that originated in French law. They assert that under the theory of administrative contracts, a
(25) government retains inherent power to modify or terminate its own contract, and that this power indeed constitutes a general principle of law. However, their argument is flawed on at least two counts.
(30)   First, in French law not all government contracts are treated as administrative contracts. Some contracts are designated as administrative by specific statute, in which case the contractor is made aware of the applicable legal rules upon
(35) entering into agreement with the government. Alternatively, the contracting government agency can itself designate a contract as administrative by including certain terms not found in private civil contracts. Moreover, even in the case of
(40) administrative contracts, French law requires that in the event that the government unilaterally modifies the terms of the contract, it must compensate the contractor for any increased burden resulting from the government's action. In
(45) effect, the government is thus prevented from modifying those contractual terms that define the financial balance of the contract.
    Second, the French law of administrative contracts, although adopted by several countries, is
(50) not so universally accepted that it can be embraced

as a general principle of law. In both the United States and the United Kingdom, government contracts are governed by the ordinary law of contracts, with the result that the government can
(55) reserve the power to modify or terminate a contract unilaterally only by writing such power into the contract as a specific provision. Indeed, the very fact that termination and modification clauses are commonly found in government contracts suggests
(60) that a government's capacity to modify or terminate agreements unilaterally derives from specific contract provisions, not from inherent state power.

1. In the passage, the author is primarily concerned with doing which one of the following?

    (A) pointing out flaws in an argument provided in support of a position
    (B) analyzing the weaknesses inherent in the proposed solution to a problem
    (C) marshaling evidence in support of a new explanation of a phenomenon
    (D) analyzing the risks inherent in adopting a certain course of action
    (E) advocating a new approach to a problem that has not been solved by traditional means

2. It can be inferred from the passage that the author would be most likely to agree with which one of the following assertions regarding the "general principles of law" mentioned in lines 16–17 of the passage?

    (A) They fail to take into account the special needs and interests of developing countries that enter into agreements with foreign investors.
    (B) They have only recently been invoked as criteria for adjudicating disputes between governments and foreign investors.
    (C) They are more compatible with the laws of France and the United States than with those of the United Kingdom.
    (D) They do not assert that governments have an inherent right to modify unilaterally the terms of agreements that they have entered into with foreign investors.
    (E) They are not useful in adjudicating disputes between developing countries and foreign investors.

GO ON TO THE NEXT PAGE.

3. The author implies that which one of the following is true of economic development agreements?

(A) They provide greater economic benefits to the governments that are parties to such agreements than to foreign investors.

(B) They are interpreted differently by courts in the United Kingdom than they are by courts in the United States.

(C) They have proliferated in recent years as a result of governments' attempts to make them more legally secure.

(D) They entail greater risk to investors when the governments that enter into such agreements reserve the right to modify unilaterally the terms of the agreements.

(E) They have become less attractive to foreign investors as an increasing number of governments that enter into such agreements consider them governed by the law of ordinary contracts.

4. According to the author, which one of the following is true of a contract that is designated by a French government agency as an administrative contract?

(A) It requires the government agency to pay for unanticipated increases in the cost of delivering the goods and services specified in the contract.

(B) It provides the contractor with certain guarantees that are not normally provided in private civil contracts.

(C) It must be ratified by the passage of a statute.

(D) It discourages foreign companies from bidding on the contract.

(E) It contains terms that distinguish it from a private civil contract.

5. It can be inferred from the passage that under the "ordinary law of contracts" (lines 53–54), a government would have the right to modify unilaterally the terms of a contract that it had entered into with a foreign investor if which one of the following were true?

(A) The government undertook a greater economic risk by entering into the contract than did the foreign investor.

(B) The cost to the foreign investor of abiding by the terms of the contract exceeded the original estimates of such costs.

(C) The modification of the contract did not result in any increased financial burden for the investor.

(D) Both the government and the investor had agreed to abide by the general principles of law recognized by civilized nations.

(E) The contract contains a specific provision allowing the government to modify the contract.

6. In the last paragraph, the author refers to government contracts in the United States and the United Kingdom primarily in order to

(A) cite two governments that often reserve the right to modify unilaterally contracts that they enter into with foreign investors

(B) support the assertion that there is no general principle of law governing contracts between private individuals and governments

(C) cast doubt on the alleged universality of the concept of administrative contracts

(D) provide examples of legal systems that might benefit from the concept of administrative contracts

(E) provide examples of characteristics that typically distinguish government contracts from private civil contracts

7. Which one of the following best states the author's main conclusion in the passage?

(A) Providing that an international agreement be governed by general principles of law is not a viable method of guaranteeing the legal security of such an agreement.

(B) French law regarding contracts is significantly different from those in the United States and the United Kingdom.

(C) Contracts between governments and private investors in most nations are governed by ordinary contract law.

(D) An inherent power of a government to modify or terminate a contract cannot be considered a general principle of law.

(E) Contracts between governments and private investors can be secured only by reliance on general principles of law.

8. The author's argument in lines 57–62 would be most weakened if which one of the following were true?

(A) The specific provisions of government contracts often contain explicit statements of what all parties to the contracts already agree are inherent state powers.

(B) Governments are more frequently put in the position of having to modify or terminate contracts than are private individuals.

(C) Modification clauses in economic development agreements have frequently been challenged in international tribunals by foreign investors who were a party to such agreements.

(D) The general principles of law provide that modification clauses cannot allow the terms of a contract to be modified in such a way that the financial balance of the contract is affected.

(E) Termination and modification agreements are often interpreted differently by national courts than they are by international tribunals.

GO ON TO THE NEXT PAGE.

Nico Frijda writes that emotions are governed by a psychological principle called the "law of apparent reality": emotions are elicited only by events appraised as real, and the intensity of these
(5) emotions corresponds to the degree to which these events are appraised as real. This observation seems psychologically plausible, but emotional responses elicited by works of art raise counterexamples.

Frijda's law accounts for my panic if I am afraid
(10) of snakes and see an object I correctly appraise as a rattlesnake, and also for my identical response if I see a coiled garden hose I mistakenly perceive to be a snake. However, suppose I am watching a movie and see a snake gliding toward its victim. Surely I
(15) might experience the same emotions of panic and distress, though I know the snake is not real. These responses extend even to phenomena not conventionally accepted as real. A movie about ghosts, for example, may be terrifying to all viewers,
(20) even those who firmly reject the possibility of ghosts, but this is not because viewers are confusing cinematic depiction with reality. Moreover, I can feel strong emotions in response to objects of art that are interpretations, rather than
(25) representations, of reality: I am moved by Mozart's *Requiem*, but I know that I am not at a real funeral. However, if Frijda's law is to explain all emotional reactions, there should be no emotional response at all to aesthetic objects or events, because we know
(30) they are not real in the way a living rattlesnake is real.

Most psychologists, perplexed by the feelings they acknowledge are aroused by aesthetic experience, have claimed that these emotions are
(35) genuine, but different in kind from nonaesthetic emotions. This, however, is a descriptive distinction rather than an empirical observation and consequently lacks explanatory value. On the other hand, Gombrich argues that emotional responses to
(40) art are ersatz: art triggers remembrances of previously experienced emotions. These debates have prompted the psychologist Radford to argue that people do experience real melancholy or joy in responding to art, but that these are irrational
(45) responses precisely because people know they are reacting to illusory stimuli. Frijda's law does not help us to untangle these positions, since it simply implies that events we recognize as being represented rather than real cannot elicit emotion
(50) in the first place.

Frijda does suggest that a vivid imagination has "properties of reality"—implying, without explanation, that we make aesthetic objects or events "real" in the act of experiencing them.
(55) However, as Scruton argues, a necessary characteristic of the imaginative construction that can occur in an emotional response to art is that the person knows he or she is pretending. This is what distinguishes imagination from psychotic fantasy.

9. Which one of the following best states the central idea of the passage?

(A) The law of apparent reality fails to account satisfactorily for the emotional nature of belief.
(B) Theories of aesthetic response fail to account for how we distinguish unreasonable from reasonable responses to art.
(C) The law of apparent reality fails to account satisfactorily for emotional responses to art.
(D) Psychologists have been unable to determine what accounts for the changeable nature of emotional responses to art.
(E) Psychologists have been unable to determine what differentiates aesthetic from nonaesthetic emotional responses.

10. According to the passage, Frijda's law asserts that emotional responses to events are

(A) unpredictable because emotional responses depend on how aware the person is of the reality of an event
(B) weaker if the person cannot distinguish illusion from reality
(C) more or less intense depending on the degree to which the person perceives the event to be real
(D) more intense if the person perceives an event to be frightening
(E) weaker if the person judges an event to be real but unthreatening

11. The author suggests that Frijda's notion of the role of imagination in aesthetic response is problematic because it

(A) ignores the unselfconsciousness that is characteristic of emotional responses to art
(B) ignores the distinction between genuine emotion and ersatz emotion
(C) ignores the fact that a person who is imagining knows that he or she is imagining
(D) makes irrelevant distinctions between vivid and weak imaginative capacities
(E) suggests, in reference to the observation of art, that there is no distinction between real and illusory stimuli

GO ON TO THE NEXT PAGE.

12. The passage supports all of the following statements about the differences between Gombrich and Radford EXCEPT:

(A) Radford's argument relies on a notion of irrationality in a way that Gombrich's argument does not.

(B) Gombrich's position is closer to the position of the majority of psychologists than is Radford's.

(C) Gombrich, unlike Radford, argues that we do not have true emotions in response to art.

(D) Gombrich's argument rests on a notion of memory in a way that Radford's argument does not.

(E) Radford's argument, unlike Gombrich's, is not focused on the artificial quality of emotional responses to art.

13. Which one of the following best captures the progression of the author's argument in lines 9–31?

(A) The emotional responses to events ranging from the real to the depicted illustrate the irrationality of emotional response.

(B) A series of events that range from the real to the depicted conveys the contrast between real events and cinematic depiction.

(C) An intensification in emotional response to a series of events that range from the real to the depicted illustrates Frijda's law.

(D) A progression of events that range from the real to the depicted examines the precise nature of panic in relation to a feared object.

(E) The consistency of emotional responses to events that range from the real to the depicted challenges Frijda's law.

14. The author's assertions concerning movies about ghosts imply that all of the following statements are false EXCEPT:

(A) Movies about ghosts are terrifying in proportion to viewers' beliefs in the phenomenon of ghosts.

(B) Movies about imaginary phenomena like ghosts may be just as terrifying as movies about phenomena like snakes.

(C) Movies about ghosts and snakes are not terrifying because people know that what they are viewing is not real.

(D) Movies about ghosts are terrifying to viewers who previously rejected the possibility of ghosts because movies permanently alter the viewers' sense of reality.

(E) Movies about ghosts elicit a very different emotional response from viewers who do not believe in ghosts than movies about snakes elicit from viewers who are frightened by snakes.

15. Which one of the following statements best exemplifies the position of Radford concerning the nature of emotional response to art?

(A) A person watching a movie about guerrilla warfare irrationally believes that he or she is present at the battle.

(B) A person watching a play about a kidnapping feels nothing because he or she rationally realizes it is not a real event.

(C) A person gets particular enjoyment out of writing fictional narratives in which he or she figures as a main character.

(D) A person irrationally bursts into tears while reading a novel about a destructive fire, even while realizing that he or she is reading about a fictional event.

(E) A person who is afraid of snakes trips over a branch and irrationally panics.

GO ON TO THE NEXT PAGE.

Although bacteria are unicellular and among the simplest autonomous forms of life, they show a remarkable ability to sense their environment. They are attracted to materials they need and are
(5) repelled by harmful substances. Most types of bacteria swim very erratically; short smooth runs in relatively straight lines are followed by brief tumbles, after which the bacteria shoot off in random directions. This leaves researchers with the
(10) question of how such bacteria find their way to an attractant such as food or, in the case of photosynthetic bacteria, light, if their swimming pattern consists only of smooth runs and tumbles, the latter resulting in random changes in direction.

(15) One clue comes from the observation that when a chemical attractant is added to a suspension of such bacteria, the bacteria swim along a gradient of the attractant, from an area where the concentration of the attractant is weaker to an area
(20) where it is stronger. As they do so, their swimming is characterized by a decrease in tumbling and an increase in straight runs over relatively longer distances. As the bacteria encounter increasing concentrations of the attractant, their tendency to
(25) tumble is suppressed, whereas tumbling increases whenever they move away from the attractant. The net effect is that runs in the direction of higher concentrations of the attractant become longer and straighter as a result of the suppression of tumbling,
(30) whereas runs away from it are shortened by an increased tendency of the bacteria to tumble and change direction.

Biologists have proposed two mechanisms that bacteria might use in detecting changes in the
(35) concentration of a chemical attractant. First, a bacterium might compare the concentration of a chemical at the front and back of its cell body simultaneously. If the concentration is higher at the front of the cell, then it knows it is moving up the
(40) concentration gradient, from an area where the concentration is lower to an area where it is higher. Alternatively, it might measure the concentration at one instant and again after a brief interval, in which case the bacterium must retain a memory of the
(45) initial concentration. Researchers reasoned that if bacteria do compare concentrations at different times, then when suddenly exposed to a uniformly high concentration of an attractant, the cells would behave as if they were swimming up a concentration
(50) gradient, with long, smooth runs and relatively few tumbles. If, on the other hand, bacteria detect a chemical gradient by measuring it simultaneously at two distinct points, front and back, on the cell body, they would not respond to the jump in
(55) concentration because the concentration of the attractant in front and back of the cells, though high, would be uniform. Experimental evidence suggests that bacteria compare concentrations at different times.

16. It can be inferred from the passage that which one of the following experimental results would suggest that bacteria detect changes in the concentration of an attractant by measuring its concentration in front and back of the cell body simultaneously?

(A) When suddenly transferred from a medium in which the concentration of an attractant was uniformly low to one in which the concentration was uniformly high, the tendency of the bacteria to tumble and undergo random changes in direction increased.

(B) When suddenly transferred from a medium in which the concentration of an attractant was uniformly low to one in which the concentration was uniformly high, the bacteria exhibited no change in the pattern of their motion.

(C) When suddenly transferred from a medium in which the concentration of an attractant was uniformly low to one in which the concentration was uniformly high, the bacteria's movement was characterized by a complete absence of tumbling.

(D) When placed in a medium in which the concentration of an attractant was in some areas low and in others high, the bacteria exhibited an increased tendency to tumble in those areas where the concentration of the attractant was high.

(E) When suddenly transferred from a medium in which the concentration of an attractant was uniformly low to one that was completely free of attractants, the bacteria exhibited a tendency to suppress tumbling and move in longer, straighter lines.

GO ON TO THE NEXT PAGE.

17. It can be inferred from the passage that a bacterium would increase the likelihood of its moving away from an area where the concentration of a harmful substance is high if it did which one of the following?

(A) increased the speed at which it swam immediately after undergoing the random changes in direction that result from tumbling
(B) detected the concentration gradient of an attractant toward which it could begin to swim
(C) relied on the simultaneous measurement of the concentration of the substance in front and back of its body, rather than on the comparison of the concentration at different points in time
(D) exhibited a complete cessation of tumbling when it detected increases in the concentration of the substance
(E) exhibited an increased tendency to tumble as it encountered increasing concentrations of the substance, and suppressed tumbling as it detected decreases in the concentration of the substance

18. It can be inferred from the passage that when describing bacteria as "swimming up a concentration gradient" (lines 49–50), the author means that they were behaving as if they were swimming

(A) against a resistant medium that makes their swimming less efficient
(B) away from a substance to which they are normally attracted
(C) away from a substance that is normally harmful to them
(D) from an area where the concentration of a repellent is weaker to an area where it is completely absent
(E) from an area where the concentration of a substance is weaker to an area where it is stronger

19. The passage indicates that the pattern that characterizes a bacterium's motion changes in response to

(A) the kinds of chemical attractants present in different concentration gradients
(B) the mechanism that the bacterium adopts in determining the presence of an attractant
(C) the bacterium's detection of changes in the concentration of an attractant
(D) the extent to which neighboring bacteria are engaged in tumbling
(E) changes in the intervals of time that occur between the bacterium's measurement of the concentration of an attractant

20. Which one of the following best describes the organization of the third paragraph of the passage?

(A) Two approaches to a problem are discussed, a test that would determine which is more efficient is described, and a conclusion is made, based on experimental evidence.
(B) Two hypotheses are described, a way of determining which of them is more likely to be true is discussed, and one is said to be more accurate on the basis of experimental evidence.
(C) Two hypotheses are described, the flaws inherent in one of them are elaborated, and experimental evidence confirming the other is cited.
(D) An assertion that a species has adopted two different mechanisms to solve a particular problem is made, and evidence is then provided in support of that assertion.
(E) An assertion that one mechanism for solving a particular problem is more efficient than another is made, and evidence is then provided in support of that assertion.

21. The passage provides information in support of which one of the following assertions?

(A) The seemingly erratic motion exhibited by a microorganism can in fact reflect a mechanism by which it is able to control its movement.
(B) Biologists often overstate the complexity of simple organisms such as bacteria.
(C) A bacterium cannot normally retain a memory of a measurement of the concentration of an attractant.
(D) Bacteria now appear to have less control over their movement than biologists had previously hypothesized.
(E) Photosynthetic bacteria appear to have more control over their movement than do bacteria that are not photosynthetic.

GO ON TO THE NEXT PAGE.

Anthropologist David Mandelbaum makes a distinction between life-passage studies and life-history studies which emerged primarily out of research concerning Native Americans. Life-
(5) passage studies, he says, "emphasize the requirements of society, showing how groups socialize and enculturate their young in order to make them into viable members of society." Life histories, however, "emphasize the experiences and
(10) requirements of the individual, how the person copes with society rather than how society copes with the stream of individuals." Life-passage studies bring out the general cultural characteristics and commonalities that broadly define a culture, but are
(15) unconcerned with an individual's choices or how the individual perceives and responds to the demands and expectations imposed by the constraints of his or her culture. This distinction can clearly be seen in the autobiographies of Native American women.
(20)   For example, some early recorded autobiographies, such as *The Autobiography of a Fox Indian Woman*, a life passage recorded by anthropologist Truman Michelson, emphasizes prescribed roles. The narrator presents her story in
(25) a way that conforms with tribal expectations. Michelson's work is valuable as ethnography, as a reflection of the day-to-day responsibilities of Mesquakie women, yet as is often the case with life-passage studies, it presents little of the central
(30) character's psychological motivation. The Fox woman's life story focuses on her tribal education and integration into the ways of her people, and relates only what Michelson ultimately decided was worth preserving. The difference between the two
(35) types of studies is often the result of the amount of control the narrator maintains over the material; autobiographies in which there are no recorder-editors are far more reflective of the life-history category, for there are no outsiders shaping the
(40) story to reflect their preconceived notions of what the general cultural patterns are.
    For example, in Maria Campbell's account of growing up as a Canadian Metis who was influenced strongly, and often negatively, by the non-Native
(45) American world around her, one learns a great deal about the life of Native American women, but Campbell's individual story, which is told to us directly, is always the center of her narrative. Clearly it is important to her to communicate to the
(50) audience what her experiences as a Native American have been. Through Campbell's story of her family the reader learns of the effect of poverty and prejudice on a people. The reader becomes an intimate of Campbell the writer, sharing her pain
(55) and celebrating her small victories. Although Campbell's book is written as a life history (the dramatic moments, the frustrations, and the fears are clearly hers), it reveals much about ethnic relations in Canada while reflecting the period in
(60) which it was written.

22. Which one of the following is the most accurate expression of the main point of the passage?

(A) The contributions of life-history studies to anthropology have made life-passage studies obsolete.

(B) Despite their dissimilar approaches to the study of culture, life-history and life-passage studies have similar goals.

(C) The autobiographies of Native American women illustrate the differences between life-history and life-passage studies.

(D) The roots of Maria Campbell's autobiography can be traced to earlier narratives such as *The Autobiography of a Fox Indian Woman*.

(E) Despite its shortcomings, the life-passage study is a more effective tool than the life-history study for identifying important cultural patterns.

23. The term "prescribed roles" in line 24 of the passage refers to the

(A) function of life-passage studies in helping ethnologists to understand cultural tradition

(B) function of life-history studies in helping ethnologists to gather information

(C) way in which a subject of a life passage views himself or herself

(D) roles clearly distinguishing the narrator of an autobiography from the recorder of an autobiography

(E) roles generally adopted by individuals in order to comply with cultural demands

24. The reference to the "psychological motivation" (line 30) of the subject of *The Autobiography of a Fox Indian Woman* serves primarily to

(A) dismiss as irrelevant the personal perspective in the life-history study

(B) identify an aspect of experience that is not commonly a major focus of life-passage studies

(C) clarify the narrator's self-acknowledged purpose in relating a life passage

(D) suggest a common conflict between the goals of the narrator and those of the recorder in most life-passage studies

(E) assert that developing an understanding of an individual's psychological motivation usually undermines objective ethnography

GO ON TO THE NEXT PAGE.

25. Which one of the following statements about Maria Campbell can be inferred from material in the passage?

    (A) She was familiar with the very early history of her tribe but lacked insight into the motivations of non-Native Americans.
    (B) She was unfamiliar with Michelson's work but had probably read a number of life-passage studies about Native Americans.
    (C) She had training as a historian but was not qualified as an anthropologist.
    (D) Her family influenced her beliefs and opinions more than the events of her time did.
    (E) Her life history provides more than a record of her personal experience.

26. According to the passage, one way in which life-history studies differ from life-passage studies is that life-history studies are

    (A) usually told in the subject's native language
    (B) less reliable because they rely solely on the subject's recall
    (C) more likely to be told without the influence of an intermediary
    (D) more creative in the way they interpret the subject's cultural legacy
    (E) more representative of the historian's point of view than of the ethnographer's

27. Which one of the following pairings best illustrates the contrast between life passages and life histories?

    (A) a study of the attitudes of a society toward a mainstream religion and an analysis of techniques used to instruct members of that religious group
    (B) a study of how a preindustrial society maintains peace with neighboring societies and a study of how a postindustrial society does the same
    (C) a study of the way a military organization establishes and maintains discipline and a newly enlisted soldier's narrative describing his initial responses to the military environment
    (D) an analysis of a society's means of subsistence and a study of how its members celebrate religious holidays
    (E) a political history of a society focussing on leaders and parties and a study of how the electorate shaped the political landscape of the society

S T O P

IF YOU FINISH BEFORE TIME IS CALLED, YOU MAY CHECK YOUR WORK ON THIS SECTION ONLY.
DO NOT WORK ON ANY OTHER SECTION IN THE TEST.

SIGNATURE _____

DATE

LSAT WRITING SAMPLE TOPIC

The port city of Cedarville is considering two offers for the purchase of a large waterfront tract just within the city limits. Write an argument for one offer over the other with the following considerations in mind:

- Cedarville wants to reverse recent declines in both employment and population.
- Cedarville wants to boost its dwindling tourist industry.

Excel Glassware Company proposes to build a three-story factory on the site. It will employ 150 people and include a research laboratory. The company, part of an international conglomerate, is known for its extensive training programs and other employee benefits. Excel manufactures glassware for private and commercial use, including a world-famous line of crystal. The offer includes a promise to bring an award-winning crystal collection to be housed in a specially designed gallery built as part of a park next to the factory. Excel promises an advertising campaign promoting guided tours of the gallery and demonstrations of glassblowers at work.

Nature Life, a national conservation organization, wants to turn the site into a wildflower and animal sanctuary. The organization plans a tourist area, complete with slide shows, nature paths, and guided tours. The facility would employ a small staff of naturalists and would include a restaurant and a lodge with accommodations for 100 guests. The organization also plans to use the site as a training center and summer school for high school and college students considering a career in conservation. Since the river contains an extensive variety of marine life, including some rare and endangered species, the state university has expressed an interest in locating a branch of its research facility nearby if the sanctuary is built.

Directions:

1. Use the Answer Key on the next page to check your answers.
2. Use the Scoring Worksheet below to compute your raw score.
3. Use the Score Conversion Chart to convert your raw score into the 120-180 scale.

Scoring Worksheet

1. Enter the number of questions you answered correctly in each section.

Number Correct

SECTION I . . . . . . _____
SECTION II . . . . . _____
SECTION III . . . . . _____
SECTION IV . . . . . _____

2. Enter the sum here: _____
This is your Raw Score.

Conversion Chart
Form 3LSS16

For Converting Raw Score to the 120-180 LSAT Scaled Score

Reported Score	Raw Score Lowest	Raw Score Highest
180	98	101
179	97	97
178	96	96
177	94	95
176	93	93
175	92	92
174	91	91
173	90	90
172	88	89
171	87	87
170	86	86
169	84	85
168	83	83
167	81	82
166	80	80
165	78	79
164	77	77
163	75	76
162	73	74
161	72	72
160	70	71
159	68	69
158	67	67
157	65	66
156	63	64
155	61	62
154	60	60
153	58	59
152	56	57
151	55	55
150	53	54
149	51	52
148	50	50
147	48	49
146	46	47
145	45	45
144	43	44
143	42	42
142	40	41
141	38	39
140	37	37
139	35	36
138	34	34
137	33	33
136	31	32
135	30	30
134	29	29
133	27	28
132	26	26
131	25	25
130	24	24
129	23	23
128	22	22
127	21	21
126	20	20
125	19	19
124	18	18
123	—*	—*
122	17	17
121	16	16
120	0	15

*There is no raw score that will produce this scaled score for this form.

SECTION I

1.	E	8.	B	15.	A	22.	C
2.	A	9.	A	16.	B	23.	B
3.	B	10.	C	17.	D	24.	C
4.	A	11.	D	18.	B	25.	E
5.	B	12.	D	19.	C		
6.	E	13.	E	20.	B		
7.	A	14.	A	21.	E		

SECTION II

1.	C	8.	B	15.	C	22.	A
2.	D	9.	B	16.	D	23.	E
3.	E	10.	B	17.	B	24.	E
4.	E	11.	D	18.	B		
5.	C	12.	B	19.	C		
6.	E	13.	B	20.	C		
7.	A	14.	C	21.	D		

SECTION III

1.	C	8.	C	15.	C	22.	E
2.	B	9.	C	16.	B	23.	D
3.	E	10.	A	17.	A	24.	B
4.	E	11.	C	18.	A	25.	E
5.	B	12.	C	19.	E		
6.	A	13.	D	20.	B		
7.	E	14.	B	21.	C		

SECTION IV

1.	A	8.	A	15.	D	22.	C
2.	D	9.	C	16.	B	23.	E
3.	D	10.	C	17.	E	24.	B
4.	E	11.	C	18.	E	25.	E
5.	E	12.	B	19.	C	26.	C
6.	C	13.	E	20.	B	27.	C
7.	D	14.	B	21.	A		